TAPPED OUT
BY JESUS FROM THE CAGE TO THE CROSS

RON WATERMAN

BRIDGE
LOGOS
FOUNDATION

Alachua, Florida 32615

TAPPED OUT
BY JESUS FROM THE CAGE TO THE CROSS

RON WATERMAN

Bridge-Logos
Alachua, FL 32615 USA

Tapped Out by Jesus: from the Cage to the Cross
by Ron Waterman

Web: www.tappedoutbyjesus.com

Printed in the United States of America.

Library of Congress Control Number 2011926395
International Standard Book Number: 978-1-61036-097-5

Edited by Hollee J. Chadwick

CONTENTS

1

CHAPTER

THE FIGHT

I STEPPED ONTO THE PLATFORM and peered through the smoke. To the left and right were many faces I knew. Although I had walked down the ramp into a cage 23 times before, it had been six years since doing it in front of thousands of people from my home town. The screams intensified the adrenaline already pumping though my body; the sweat dripped from my face. I stopped and said a prayer, asking the Lord to walk with me.

After days of fighting nerves and playing the fight over and over in my head, I get the greatest sense of peace just minutes before I step in the cage. I have often wondered if it hurts my performance because of the calming effect it has on my body and mind. There are still some jitters as I walk to the cage, but nothing like the days leading up to the fight.

Time seemed to stand still as I made my way down the long ramp. The steel cage was just ahead, surrounded by thousands of screaming fans, flashing lights, and misty smoke. My corner men were waiting to give me one more pep talk and hug of encouragement. At the end of the ramp I tapped my cup twice, showed my mouth guard, and had some cold petroleum jelly rubbed over my eyes and mouth. I paused before entering the cage and prayed one last time for Jesus to enter with me, comfort me, and allow me to compete at my best.

My 336-pound opponent entered the cage in a full-length bear coat, jumping up and down in a lather of his own. The Bear, as he was called, didn't quite make the 285-pound limit, but I wasn't about to cancel the fight. Coming into a fight at 336 pounds would not be an easy task for him, especially after a couple of minutes trying to breathe at Colorado's elevation. I have always taken for granted the altitude at which I train, but it really does make a difference—especially when you're a super-heavyweight fighter. I have never feared any opponent but I have feared running out of air. It doesn't matter how tough you are if you can't breathe, and unfortunately I have been close to that point a few times inside the cage. It's a nightmare.

That wouldn't be the case this time. I was confident the fight would not go three rounds, but if it did, I would be ready. As the Bear entered the cage, I stared into his eyes with confidence and determination. He tried to glare back but quickly turned his eyes away, which only increased my assurance.

The cage door slammed shut and locked in place. We were called to meet in the middle of the cage. After a brief talk, we slapped gloves and stepped back for the bell to sound. It was finally here. Two months of training four hours a day and all the sweat, blood, aches, pains, and stress that went along with it were about to be behind me.

Most don't understand the commitment that goes into three rounds. For me, training is the easy part. I study my opponents and learn what I need to do and what could be a fatal mistake. With the Internet it's also easy for my opponents to watch any of my previous fights to discover my strengths and weaknesses. Mixed Martial Arts (MMA) is a game of chess, especially in this day and age. The stereotype of barroom brawlers out to show how tough they are is hardly true today. The MMA fighter is well-rounded, trained in three or four arts and deadly in all of them. Weekend warriors in MMA don't last long and aren't given the opportunity to come back after one or two poor showings.

The next thing I knew, someone shouted "Let's get it on!" I advanced to touch gloves and make the first chess move of the night. The last place I wanted to be was under the Bear's 336 pounds, so I waited and didn't do what I did in 23 prior fights—a rush for the takedown. Instead, I stood with the Bear but stayed out of his long reach and surprisingly fast hands. I had worked on my hands and movement, circled, and landed a number of hard jabs to his jaw, but as hard as they landed, nothing seemed to faze him. He stayed on the defensive, waiting for me to shoot in and take my patent double leg. Knowing time was on my side, I continued to press forward and pick up the tempo of punches. The Bear's breathing quickened, as he tried to get in more of that thin Colorado air. A fast jab of his own caught me on the mouth and I was reminded not to get over-confident, to keep my hands up, and to wait for him to make a mistake. A few more flurries of punches and kicks and the first five minutes had already gone by. I felt good, and my lungs were where they needed to be. My brother, one of my corner men, gave me a quick drink, wiped the blood off my lip, and told me my game plan was perfect.

The second round bell always comes fast. It seemed I had just sat down on the stool when the cage slammed shut and the famous "Let's get it on!" was sounded again. Six minutes into this fight now and the Bear was getting desperate to end it any way he could. I landed a number of hard punches and he lunged for my legs, attempting to take me down. My quickness and fresh lungs made it easy to sprawl and spin behind him, land hammer fists, and look for a submission. He rolled to his side as I stepped over to full mount, posted his arm up high, and locked up an arm triangle that I'd been working on for a few weeks before the fight. I shifted my weight and walked it to the side. From the corner of my eye I could see the grimace on the Bear's face and I felt a burst of strength. I pulled in my elbows and squeezed with all I had, pushing my head into his temple for added leverage.

He reached up with his free hand and tapped my shoulder, signaling for the official to stop the fight. The feeling a person gets at that moment is almost indescribable. The months of training, the sacrifices, the diet, bad moods, and the stress become a thing of the past and a small price to have paid for the glory of the moment. I stood and immediately knew who I was to thank—not my sponsors, not my training partners, definitely not myself, but the only One who made it possible: Jesus. I looked up, pointed to the sky, and openly said, *Thank you Lord!* A huge sense of relief came over me, not just from the win, but because the moment was over.

I always like to make sure my opponent is okay, so as I was rushed by my corner men—my brother Doug and my friend Norman—with hugs and words of celebration, I made my way back across the cage to check the status of my opponent. Pale and breathing heavily, he complimented my condition and thanked me for the opportunity to fight. I have never competed against an opponent I had bad feelings for; on the contrary, I respect them and want them to know that.

In the Ultimate Fighting Championship (UFC) 23, I fought an all-out war with Tim Lacik. It was the first time I had ever gone the distance in a fight— three five-minute rounds—and I did it with a completely severed right bicep. I had torn it off the bone exactly one week prior to the fight while practicing at Colorado Stars in Denver. I took down one of my partners in the room and felt a funny snap. The next morning I found out my bicep was completely detached. It had rolled up my arm almost to my shoulder.

It was only my third UFC fight and I was not about to back out of the opportunity to fight on Pay-Per-View against the fighter many thought would be the next UFC Heavyweight Champion. A point was deducted in the fight for a low punch that changed the scorecard to a Draw. It's funny to watch this fight and see my right bicep in that rolled up position.

The next morning Tim and I arrived at the airport at the same time. It turned out that not only were we on the same flight, we had seats right next to one another. The plane was so small that I had to duck to walk down the aisle. I looked at over at Tim and grinned at his cut lip and swollen black eyes. He had the same grin on his face as he looked at my eye swollen shut and my arm, three times its normal size, in a sling. We laughed and had a great flight back. Tim and I were both school teachers as well as fighters. I'm sure we had the same questions from students when we went back into the classroom looking like we'd been in a car wreck.

I had my bicep reattached and had to rehab it for five months, but it came back stronger than the other. Praise God it's the only serious injury I have had in 11 years of fighting.

BIG JAB TO THE BEAR

11

FIGHT POSE

GIVING THE PRAISE TO JESUS

TOUCH OF CLASS

ENJOYING THE VICTORY

YOU'RE A CHRISTIAN?

IN HUNDREDS OF INTERVIEWS and conversations on the street, the question I've been asked most is, "How can you be a Christian and do what you do?" My answer is simple—it's a sport, a competition, no different than football, hockey, boxing, or any other sporting event. I don't compete to show how strong or tough I am. I don't do it for recognition or status and there wasn't much money in it in the beginning. I do it because I like to compete, and know I can do it and be who I am—a Christian in a sport surrounded by fighters who need to know Jesus and need all the Christian examples they can get. If God can use me to be an example in this world, in this sport, in this environment, why would I say no?

I was given the microphone after fighting the Bear. I wasn't about to tell the world where the after-party was. I wasn't going to throw out *f-bombs* every other word and tell everyone how good I was and that no one could ever beat me. That's just not me. My victory didn't come because Ron Waterman was a stud, but because the Lord allowed me to win and gave me the ability to win. Why would I even try to take the credit?

Instead, I stood in the middle of the cage and let the entire coliseum know that Jesus Christ gets the glory and praise. I don't say that to get a pat on the back. I thank the Lord because He is worthy of my praise. My life verse is Joshua 1:9 *"Have I not commanded you? Be strong and courageous. Do not be terrified; do not be discouraged, for the Lord your God will be with you wherever you go."* I can't tell you how many times I have used this verse in my life—sometimes many times a day. It's not just used to comfort me for a fight but to comfort me in everyday life. It gives me comfort against the world.

As I write this book and think about all the different chapters of my life, it amazes me how much God is in control. He decides to change the chapter of life I am in and send me in a direction I had no idea I would ever go. Oftentimes I feel like I have my life totally in control and set on a good path and it's suddenly changed and I'm on a path I don't understand or like. Other times in my life I am distraught and confused and not content with where my life is headed and the Lord suddenly makes things clear to me, straightens that path and makes my way perfect.

The one thing I have come to understand in the last ten years as a Christian is that God is in control and I'm not. There are plenty of times I forget this, especially when things are going great— the money is coming in, the bills are paid, my relationships are going smoothly, and my boys are excelling in life. That isn't often the way life goes, but at times it does. I have friends who are financially set with not a worry in the world. They can buy anything they want at any time of the day.

There is nothing wrong with a person who has worked hard and made a comfortable life for himself and his family. Most of my wealthy friends are extremely generous with their money and are blessed because of their cheerful giving. It's when money is used selfishly or takes over a person's life that it's dangerous.

Jesus was talking to His disciples about this in Matthew 19:23-24, *"I tell you the truth it is hard for a rich man to enter the kingdom of Heaven."* And in verse 24, He makes an analogy *"Again I tell you, it is easier for a camel to go through the eye of a needle than for a rich man to enter the kingdom of God."* A rich man could easily struggle with God, not thinking he needs Him.

I see many trying to purchase their happiness—a new car, new house, new clothes and jewelry—it's a never-ending cycle. I would be a liar if I claimed to only *know* of people like this, but that I was much different early in my career. I was never in the position to go out and purchase everything I wanted, but there was definitely a time when I tried to fill the void with stuff. I had the half-million dollar house, the hundred thousand dollar Hummer, and lots of nice toys to go with it all. Fortunately, God didn't allow me to stay in that chapter of my life for very long.

The Bible tells us in Luke 16:10-12, *"Whoever can be trusted with very little can also be trusted with much, and whoever is dishonest with very little will also be dishonest with much. So if you have not been trustworthy in handling worldly wealth, who will trust you with true riches? And if you have not been trustworthy with someone else's property, who will give you property of your own?"* That verse really made sense to me and if nothing else it scared me enough to realize that I was not being a good steward of my money and it could be taken away as fast as it was earned. And it was, more than once.

3

CHAPTER

CRAVE VIDEO GAME

AFTER I HAD BEEN FIGHTING less than two years in the UFC, a gaming company called Crave Entertainment was starting production of the first UFC video game. The UFC contacted me and asked if I would be interested in being one of the fighters in the game for Sega Dreamcast® and PlayStation®. I was not about to say *no* to the offer, but didn't know what to expect. I was told they needed to fly me to California and put me through a series of photographs, record sound bites, and hook up little magnets all over my body as I went through a series of motions. They had a crew who studied my fights and learned my motions, moves, and even facial expressions. The greatest move of all was me kneeling and praying after the fight ends. It was amazing to see them work and the way their minds functioned—not like mine, that's for sure.

Being selected for the video game wasn't the reason that God had me flying this particular day. He sat me next to a man named Jeff Bolin. Jeff started up a conversation with me after some time and told me I looked like Stone Cold Steve Austin. Not the first time I had heard that remark, but I smiled and shrugged it off. Jeff continued to ask questions until I ended up explaining to him what I did and why I was going to California. It turned out that Jeff was good friends with Shane McMahon— yes, the son of World Wrestling Entertainment's (WWE) Vince McMahon. (It was the World Wrestling Foundation, or WWF, at that time.) We talked the rest of the flight and I told him that the WWE had always been a childhood dream of mine, but one I never really had the opportunity to pursue. I was married my senior year of college, had two incredible boys soon after, and became a teacher and coach. So how was I ever to pursue a childhood dream of being a professional wrestler?

I took Jeff's business card and gave him one of my own. We stayed in touch and Jeff set up a meeting with Jim Ross, the WWF developmental talent scout, and Shane at the WWF headquarters in Stamford, Connecticut. I'd previously looked into professional wrestling through my agent and manager, Phyllis Lee, who was a former professional wrestler herself back in the day. She had a training opportunity lined up for me in Memphis, Tennessee that I was contemplating. The following month, my new friend Jeff, who had been working in Denver, was hired by Shane McMahon and moved his family to Connecticut to work at the corporate office. I quickly put together a resume.

When I arrived and stood outside the complex, it all seemed somewhat surreal. I walked in with Jeff and was shown around the building. There was even some time to kill, so I worked out in a state of the art weight room that the employees and Vince trained in daily. As I showered, I sparked up a conversation with a friendly guy they called "Coach." Yes, that would be Jonathan Coachman, a great guy who always went out of his way to say *hi* in the following years.

This was the easy part. The hard part came next.

4

BIG TIME, SMALL FISH

I LIVED IN COLORADO with my wife and two young boys. How was I going to pull them out of school for six months while I trained? I really didn't want to sell the dream house we'd built only a few years earlier.

I decided to do it on my own: fly back and forth for three to six months until my training was done and then fly from Denver to my WWF matches every week. I will never forget the feeling I had that day. My car was packed, and there was nothing left to do but say goodbye to my wife and boys and pursue a childhood dream of being a professional wrestler.

I didn't know how long it would take, I didn't know what to expect, and I didn't know what would be expected of me. I was soon to find out.

One thing I was expecting was that I would pull up to a state-of-the-art training facility with someone ready to hand me a towel and water bottle as I walked through the door. But, as I approached Danny Davis's wrestling school, I was sure I was lost in the wrong part of town. This was certainly not the training facility that I was going to become a "professional" in! It was an industrial building that looked like it should have been long ago condemned.

I met Danny in a small office, cluttered with videotapes and equipment. He was short and stocky—the classic old school wrestler profile. Danny had a bit of a temper, but he was a great guy and never treated me with anything but respect. He called a few of the developmental talents performing that night into his office.

First was a guy named Russ McCullough, a seven-foot monster resembling Kevin Nash, long hair and all. Next was a familiar face, Sylvester Terkay. I'd wrestled Sylvester in the Olympic Trials in Las Vegas a few years earlier. He was much larger than I remembered, at 6' 5" and 310 pounds. Wow, it had been a long time since I felt so small. My big-fish-in-a-small-pond days were over.

Russ was asked to show me around and introduce me to the rest of the boys in the back. We walked into a small locker room that smelled of baby oil, cooking spray, and smelly knee pads. I was a little surprised to see 12 wrestlers in this tiny room, changing right alongside a handful of women. It didn't even faze them. Russ introduced me to some guys who I ended up becoming very close to and was to spend a chapter of my life with.

5

CHAPTER

FREAK SHOW

THE OHIO VALLEY WRESTLING SCHOOL (OVW), located in Louisville, Kentucky, was comprised of developmental talent like me, who were under a WWF contract, and local wrestlers trying to land a WWE contract. Most had very little chance of that ever happening, not because they weren't good workers, but because they didn't have the physical gifts needed to be a TV talent. They were boys amongst men.

Dave Batista (Leviathan) a 6' 4" former bodybuilder with veins bigger than some of the guys' arms, was among the new talent. John Cena was also there, one of the most gifted talkers I have ever heard and another physically-gifted guy. There was Shelton Benjamin, a former Minnesota wrestler who ate Pringles potato chips, drank pop, and was one of the most gifted natural athletes I've seen. I was introduced to a young, somewhat cocky kid named Randy Orton whose dad was a superstar in the business, "Cowboy Bob Orton." It was obvious Randy grew up around the sport as his ring skills came very naturally.

I felt like I had landed on a different planet. I was born and raised in Greeley, Colorado and had spent my entire life there. I was in a place I wasn't prepared for in many ways. The physical part of OVW was not an issue after being a wrestler my entire life and going through practices that the average person couldn't even comprehend. OVW was intense with two practices a day most days, and matches at night where we not only drove to the venue but also had to set up the ring and chairs and everything else that went along with the production. Not really what I expected, but it was a learning experience. The developmental talent was the group responsible for all of this because we were the ones being paid for it. The other wrestlers showed up a little before the match to review the night's show, and left right after. We stayed and broke down the ring, folded chairs, and cleaned up. The next day we did it all over again.

The mental aspect of the situation I was put in—being so far from my family and everything I knew—put me over the edge and left me broken. I tried to remember the words of Paul when he wrote in Romans 8:18, *"Our present sufferings are not worth comparing with the glory that will be revealed to us."*

The OVW wrestlers had a number of perks in Louisville. We could eat free at a number of establishments, were able to see movies anytime for free, were given free gym memberships, and were treated like royalty most of the time. As I said, most OVW talent didn't look like the typical guy walking down the street. They stood out in a crowd and drew attention almost everywhere they went. It was interesting to see how the boys dealt with fans outside the arena. It tells a lot about a person to see how they treat others, especially Kentucky fans.

Only a short time had passed and the arrival of the much-talked-about new talent showed up at Danny Davis Arena— Brock Lesnar. To most, Brock was a little on the arrogant side, but he made a good impression with me and was very respectful. What I admired most about Brock was his attitude towards hard work. I could tell he grew up on a farm and was no stranger to blood and sweat. After one practice I could pick out every former wrestler in that locker room—they just stand out from everyone else.

6

CHAPTER

THE CHALLENGE

IT DIDN'T TAKE LONG to get called out in the testosterone-filled arena. After only a couple practices, one of the most thickly-built individuals I'd ever laid eyes on called me up into the ring before practice and wanted to see what I had. The whole incident was egged on by another developmental talent named "Slick Robbie D," a good guy I ended up being great friends with. Mark Henry, whose WWF name at the time was "Sexual Chocolate" had been a WWF TV talent for some time. He was dubbed the "world's strongest man" after winning a strongman competition. He was crazy strong, big, and heavy, which was the reason he was in OVW. He had to get off some weight and get more ring time before being called back to the traveling WWF roster.

Who was I to back down? All the boys knew my background as a UFC fighter, so of course the crowd gathered quickly around the ring. Mark made sure I wouldn't hit him and I smiled as I grabbed that thick neck of his. I quickly slammed his 400 pounds of muscle to the canvas as Slick and all the boys began to pop[1]. Mark was on his back and I was attempting to submit him with a *chook* but before I knew it I was three feet in the air. He bench pressed me straight up! Wow, that was a new feeling! After a short tussle, I took Mark's back and he tapped out from exhaustion more than anything else. I think I won some respect from Mark that day, but more than that from the boys who stood and watched.

Brock and I ended up becoming pretty close friends and lived in the same apartment complex only a few doors away. We spent a good deal of time together aside from the two-a-day practices and evening matches. We trained together every day at a couple different gyms, which was nice because I hadn't met many people I could lift with who would stay consistent, work hard, and be the accountability I needed. Brock and I were similar in strength and close to the same weight, so it was a good fit for training. We both ate like horses and tried to keep it clean most of the time.

The one thing I respected more than anything else was that Brock knew the Lord. He gave his life to Jesus in college and had no problem talking about that experience. Being a fairly new Christian, I needed all the good influences I could find. Proverbs 27:17 says, *"As iron sharpens iron, so one man sharpens another."* OVW and professional wrestling is not an easy place for any Christian to survive, let alone a new believer.

Brock and I spent a good majority of our free time together: meals, errands, movies, and just hanging out at the mall. It's odd how Brock and I were so alike in some aspects of our lives but so different in others. We drew attention everywhere we went, some good and some bad. Ninety percent of the time it was just lookers and gawkers. Some wanted to know who we were and wanted something signed or a picture. Others just wanted to start up a conversation and ask questions like "how

---

1   Yell out and get excited.

much can you lift?" or "what do you bench?" and then proceed to tell us about their training regimen. I was always nice and smiled and listened. Brock, on the other hand, was not usually so kind. He would tell them the key to getting big is eating 13 Snickers bars a day or a dozen bananas. He would just come up with something off the top of his head just to get them out of his face, and most believed him.

7

CHAPTER

I GET PAID TO DO THIS?

THIS WAS THE FIRST TIME in my life I was being paid to work out. Sounds like a perfect life, doesn't it? Not really. It was one of the most difficult years of my life. We had a rigorous regimen, with an intense two-hour practice inside the ring each morning, followed by a night-time show three or four nights a week. We had one home house show each week at Davis Arena, then another in a church gymnasium, and then on weekends we would often travel for hours and set up the ring for another house show.

Personal training was on our own. Mine was typically an hour-and-a-half of weight training followed by an hour of cardiovascular work. Much of this business is about selling yourself, so the better you look and the better shape you're in, the better your chances of making it. I was used to this kind of training from wrestling all those years plus training a couple hours every day for years in my hometown gym. Taking care of my body was one of the easiest tasks for me, and it didn't seem to be that big of a deal. As I looked around the locker room I noticed it was a big deal for many others—mostly the local talent—but there were others, even some under contract, who had a hard time keeping fit and looking the part.

Many of the developmental talents[2] were naturally freaky big guys given physical gifts from the Lord. Not that they didn't have to work hard to maintain those gifts; most of these guys were coming out of other professional sports or collegiate backgrounds so they had backgrounds similar to mine. I had to remind myself that I was now being paid and being paid well for doing what I always had done—train.

My diet was also a big part of what I had to maintain. At this level I had to eat and eat well. I had to force myself to put protein in my body when I was full and really didn't want to eat. I was cooking for myself now so I had no one to blame for not getting the right amount of nutrition in my body.

After most mid-morning practices a lot of the guys would go out to eat together for lunch. We had to be careful because we weren't supposed to be seen in public with a rival in the ring. If we were caught in public hanging out with someone we were having a feud with, we were reprimanded in the office!

It was usually a spectacle wherever we'd go, as nine or ten 300-pound wrestlers walked into Qdoba or another restaurant to grab lunch. The attention was usually the same: little kids would come up and ask for autographs, mothers would gawk and fathers wouldn't make eye contact. "How much can you bench" always seemed to come up. Fans and admirers were a part of the business and something we had to get used to.

I was always reminded of Jeremiah 9:23-24, *"Let not the wise man boast of his wisdom or the strong man boast of his strength or the rich man boast of his riches, but let him who boasts boast*

---

2   A wrestler with a WWE contract who hasn't been called up to the traveling roster yet.

about this: that he understands and knows me, that I am the Lord, who exercises kindness, justice and righteousness on earth, for in these I delight."

Most of the boys did a good job handling the fame, but even the nicest of guys would occasionally get their patience tested. People would walk up in the middle of a meal and want to talk. They'd tell us about their workout programs and ask questions about how we got so big, or tell us about how they used to be athletes and in great shape. Week after week we had a similar routine, traveling to different towns on the weekends, setting up the ring, tearing down the ring, and putting out the chairs. It was interesting as I reflect back on all the different places I worked and some of the bizarre venues I was in. Many of the bars we would set the ring up in we couldn't do any high flying maneuvers because the roof was right above the ring. Smoke and the smell of alcohol filled the room. We would change in a back room, oil up, and warm up before walking out to the screaming crowds.

I was always amazed at how fans really got into these matches and the wrestlers. If you were a *heel* (the bad guy) you were hated and lucky to get out of the building, for real. If you were a *face* (the good guy) they cheered at the top of their lungs and cried for you and waited to touch your hand as you left the ring.

It was nice that Danny Davis and Jim Cornette would match our characters with our personality most of the time as it was just easier to be who you really are as a person in the ring, only magnified for the show. I was a much better face than a heel. It was a much easier fit and transition for me to be a good guy even if I was coming in as an Ultimate Fighter. I was intense, physical, and powerful, but almost always a nice guy. I enjoyed the fans cheering and chanting my name for my comeback. I liked to sign autographs after the shows and talk to fans, despite the monotony.

I GET PAID TO DO THIS?

8

CHAPTER

FIRST LESSONS
AND GOOD INTENTIONS

MY INTENTIONS WERE GOOD. I made sure everyone knew I was a believer and that I was unashamed to say so. I befriended everyone I met and really disliked no one. Most OVW wrestlers, both on contract and locals, were good people, but lost and living for the world. I can't say one bad thing about them because as much as I wanted to make a statement for the Lord and live as He would have me live in that dark environment, I found myself no different than the rest.

Three months of practice quickly turned into six, and six months turned into a year. What I thought would be a fast transition from my collegiate background was a long, drawn-out political nightmare. My visits home had become less often and my relationship with my wife and two boys had started to crumble right under my feet. My big chance of chasing a childhood dream was not as exciting as I expected and certainly wasn't worth the price—my soul.

A year of training and looking out for no one but me was taking its toll; even the telephone calls home at night were just not the same. I knew something had to happen fast, before I lost my family. I had given up a teaching and coaching position to chase this dream. I missed a year of my boys' lives, school functions, and sporting events. I had no idea what the Lord was doing or planning for my life. I was not at peace and always wondered if the day would come when I would be called up to the traveling roster and be able to move back home and live the life I had dreamed about for so long. I knew it still would not be a cake walk with the WWF traveling roster and the time I would be away from home, but at least I would live at home and see my family every week.

Life in OVW was difficult in many ways. We had the constant pressure of "making it" to the next level. Weekly tapes of our performances were sent up to Titan towers for review, as well as our matches and practice interviews. After some of the talent had been around for six months and the office didn't see big signs of improvement, the talent would get a call and get his pink slip—he was being cut from his developmental contract. Every month cuts would come out and we would find out who was headed home or to the independent circuit to try to make it on their own.

Oftentimes we were surprised by who was being sent home, while others were obvious. Sylvester Terkay, a great guy and a Division 1 wrestling runner-up to Kurt Angle, was one of the cuts that came as a surprise to most of the guys. Sylvester was a great Christian with high morals and standards.

"Slick Robbie D," on contract from Memphis, was another they let go after some time. Robbie ended up being a good friend of mine. A short while after he was let go he had a run-in with the law. All the guys were sat down at practice one day and told that Robbie had taken his own life in jail by hanging himself. I was floored at the news. I could picture Robbie and his sense of humor so well. Robbie had asked me to draw a picture of him when he found out I was an art major in college. I drew one of him in his wrestling outfit and it turned out really good. I hope I get to see Robbie again someday in heaven. He spoke of the Lord now and then, but I never really talked to him about his salvation.

After 15 months the call finally came that I was going to begin traveling with WWF doing dark matches. These are the matches that happen before television taping begins. There would be two or three of them every night, to see how the crowd reacted to the new talent, for Vince and the office boys to see where their ability was, and to see how the veteran wrestlers liked working with them. That was a much bigger part of being accepted and being called up to a permanent position than we realized.

I was quickly identified as a *shooter*. A shooter is a wrestler who has a background as a fighter, collegiate wrestler—anyone with a firm wrestling style. I spent my entire life in one-on-one physical competition and as a UFC fighter, so that kind of speaks for itself.

Many of the boys in the back didn't want to work with a shooter, especially a new, inexperienced one. This was their living, and as a Pro Wrestler you depend on your partner to keep you safe, not to mess up and allow you to fall the wrong way, or to bump you while taking your head off in the process. That was all a part of the game I had to learn.

The first time shaking wrestlers' hands they almost screamed, "Whoa, shooter, easy, easy!" I was always taught when you shake someone's hand to shake it nice and firm—a man's handshake. Not so in professional wrestling. A firm handshake means a stiff wrestler. From that point on, my handshake was a mere light touch. Now I was a worker, not a shooter. One lesson learned, with many yet to come.

The next lesson to be learned was to never ignore a wrestler in the room, especially a veteran. You walk up and shake their hand and acknowledge them right away, even if they don't know you. It only takes one time for you to forget and then you get the tag of being too good, cocky, or just disrespectful, and that's not a good thing when you're trying to become one of the boys.

9
CHAPTER

DARK MATCHES

I HAD NEVER SEEN ANYTHING LIKE IT. As I walked into the arena for my first dark match it was almost a surreal experience. I was entering with the superstars of the WWF I'd watched on TV while growing up. I walked into the locker room with "The Rock," "The Undertaker," "Stone Cold Steve Austin," and the rest of the WWF talent all around me. I made my rounds, shook hands, and made it look as if I was just another one of the boys. All the while, I was very nervous and not sure what move to make next, thinking about my first impressions in and out of the ring. One of the stresses in Pro Wrestling I never really became accustomed to was not knowing who I was going to face that night, often until right before the show. For the veteran wrestlers, it was just another day. They were used to working with all the talent on the roster, had a somewhat typical routine, and just needed a few minutes to piece it together. But as a rookie, I was usually nervous, and afraid to mess up a spot, lay in a punch, or not sell a move like I should have.

I was matched up with a guy named Steve Bradley for my first dark match, another up-and-comer wrestler who had been around for a while and was a very good worker. I was pleased with how easy it was to talk and work with Steve. He was picked to be the "heel" that particular night and he made me look like a hero. It was one of the better matches I can remember having, and in front of my first really big crowd. I came back into the locker room that night and received a number of positive reviews from the WWF agents and wrestlers. Johnny Ace was my agent for the match and had many others looking on for their thoughts on my performance. Arn Anderson came up to me and told me I had a natural stage presence that couldn't be taught, and it made me feel pretty good.

After the match I was quickly booked on the next several dark matches and would fly out to shows every week. Little did I know my next dark match would be viewed by Vince McMahan himself. I was set to face "Scotty Too Hotty," a great guy who was always a crowd favorite, so I was to be the heel. Scotty had several TV spots and interviews to get done before the show started. so we had very little time to work out our match. A few spots and we called it good.

The match went fine until a spot I was sure I did correctly was turned around by Scotty. We made adjustments that made me look pretty bad. Subsequently my first impression on many was not so good. I put him over[3] at the end, which I was supposed to do, but he ended up slamming me twice and I'm much bigger, so it looked a little odd.

I should've had much more offense and aggression. One thing you don't do is talk negative about your partner in the ring, especially when it's a veteran who's been around much longer and is popular with the crowd. So I took the criticism and tried to make my next match better.

---

3   Helping the other wrestler look good in the match, usually with a win.

Weekly dark matches turned into months and I was becoming a little more at ease around the boys. The most exciting part was that I was able to move back home to Colorado. I felt like I'd finally made it, no more OVW, no more daily practices and setting up the ring before shows. No more phone calls home to my family. It was all falling back into place after over a year of serious life tests. I was still flying out every Friday but the two or three days at home were nice. Seeing my boys and wife every week made all the difference to me.

After traveling for a few months I became pretty good friends with Shane McMahon. He was always very interested in my progress and often gave me pointers on what he thought would get me over. He was also a big fan of MMA, so when I would show some of the boys a few submissions in the ring before the doors opened, he would always be the first to want to learn some new moves. Of course, some of the boys wanted to know if I was for real, and like Mark Henry did in OVW, some wanted to challenge me. I ended up rolling with a handful of the boys and gained some respect after tapping most of them at will regardless of how big they were. The guys who didn't want to get in the ring and roll were all watching from the outside most of the time. I think some of the guys still had that fear that I was a shooter and was going to be a stiff wrestler. I wasn't around long enough to really get to know most of the guys. It really is a tight group and you're either in or you're out with most of them.

Taker and the Dudley Boys would always play cards when they got to the venues. I was amazed at how relaxed they all were, but after doing it for years I'm sure I would have been the same. Just another day at the office, for them.

My brain was automatically wondering who I was going to be matched up with that night and when my match would be. Then I'd start worrying about my match and if I would have enough time to work out a good match. I needed more time to prepare myself than most guys did who had been in the business for years. I had to rehearse it in my mind over and over before I was comfortable.

The stress and pressure of dark matches was intense because we were under a microscope, not only with the office and Vince but with the boys in the back who were more critical than anyone. Some would give you pointers after the match, others were like high school girls, talking about everything you did wrong to the boys behind your back and not to your face.

There were a few of the guys who I just never felt comfortable with—I guess that's normal with a large group of testosterone-filled men. I'm sure Pro Football teams have guys who feel the same way; some just don't get along and their personalities clash. I am a pretty laid-back guy and get along with just about everyone. I didn't care for guys who used filthy language and had cocky attitudes. Some of the old timers would always say to keep it real, meaning don't let this job go to your head. It was usually the guys who were not over-the-top superstars who had the big heads and egos.

I had been chasing a dream and had good intentions, but many decisions I made were very selfish and without consideration for my family. What I thought was about to be the opportunity of a lifetime ended up being a setback in my life with serious repercussions. After four months of dark matches and traveling from home to various locations around the United States, I was notified that the writers had nothing for me and I was being released. I think that was just a nice way of saying the famous Donald Trump line from *The Apprentice*, "You're fired!"

I wasn't used to failing at anything, and took it really hard. The WWE doesn't go into detail about why you're being let go, just a nice phone call saying that the writers don't have anything for you. What does that mean? It drove me nuts! I gave up a 10-year teaching position at a high school to pursue this dream and now they don't have anything for me? I gave up over two years of my life for this? Now what?

HELPING WWF'S BOBBY EATON FLY

10

CHAPTER

JESUS HAD
A FEW IDEAS

WHEN GOD CLOSES A DOOR He always opens a window. I didn't understand it at the time, but looking back it's clear. I was not meant to be in that environment. Being a new Christian, I was not prepared to face that lifestyle with its temptations. Jesus had a rope around me and allowed me to run but knew when I needed to be pulled back in and not allowed to go any further. Praise Jesus!

I had no idea what direction I was to go: back to teaching, back to fighting, a new career? So many questions, so few answers. One thing I did know was that I had to renew my commitment to Jesus and get closer to the One who already knew what direction I was to take next. I prayed long and hard day after day. I was worried about my career and how I would support It was difficult to go back to an ordinary lifestyle. I was used to being treated like a celebrity. Now I was back home without a job or income and had no idea what I was to do next with my life.

Rico Constantino was one of the OVW talents I met and respected and one of the only wrestlers older than me. He was an American Gladiator Champion who had done many things in his life up to that point and had some amazing stories to share. One of his previous jobs really got my attention. He was a member of a group called the Power Team. The Power Team was a Christian strength team that traveled around the world doing crazy feats of strength and sharing their faith. I had no idea what the job really entailed, but I *was* impressed that he could tear a big phone book right down the middle like it was one sheet of paper. I was much bigger and stronger than Rico and there was no way I could do that. One day when I was praying, the Lord spoke to me and said to call Rico and find out more about this Christian strength team thing.

Rico talked to me for some time about the team and told me to contact a friend of his who had actually started up a new team called Team Impact (TI). He gave me the number to TI and told me it was run by two guys, Brandon Hensley and Jeff Audas, both former employees of the Power Team. I was a little nervous about calling, so I ended up writing a long email and sending it to the website, telling them about myself and about what I felt I was called to do next in my life.

Amazingly, 30 minutes later Jeff Audas called me. We had a long conversation about everything, but most importantly about my relationship with Jesus. TI is concerned about the athletes they hire to represent their ministry. Coming from the Power Team, they saw what bad character can do to the entire ministry. Jeff wanted my pastor's information and number for reference. I was also to have a phone conversation with their team chaplain, who was also the chaplain for the Dallas Cowboys. He called me the next day and soon after a flight was scheduled to fly me to Coppell, Texas to meet the team and participate in a five-day crusade in Lake Charles, Louisiana.

11

CHAPTER

TEAM IMPACT

Some of the same feelings I'd had as I walked into the OVW locker room came back to me as I met the Team Impact athletes for the first time. The first guy I met was Jeff Neal, one of the team leaders who would be running the five-day crusade I was attending. He was a former offensive lineman for the Houston Oilers and a monster as well—over 300 pounds with a big barrel chest.

Jeff floored me as we began to talk and get to know one another. I'd never been around someone like him. We seemed to connect from the start. He was a big, strong, professional athlete but had a love for Jesus I still don't know that I've witnessed in another individual. He was the most humble person I'd ever met and had reason by most people's standards not to be.

My respect for Jeff only grew as I saw the person he really was. Jeff was a Godly example to his peers and everyone who came in contact with him and is a big reason why Team Impact is what it is. To this day I've never heard anyone preach and tell a story like he can. I continue to try to model my speaking after Jeff, and hope one day to be half the communicator he is.

I had no idea what I was really getting into, nor did I know what would be expected of me during the next five days. I wanted to make a good impression and give 100 percent in all I did. I felt very comfortable around the guys, especially after traveling with the WWE. This was a bright light after coming out of a dark tunnel. The pride and egos I was used to dealing with, looking the other way, tuning out poor language, and trying to look past poor choices was not a part of Team Impact. This was different, much different. This was so real, so refreshing, and so different from anything I'd experienced in my entire life. I felt like God had me where He wanted me.

I was teamed up with Guy Earl, a former lineman on the Washington Redskins. On Team Impact, to save money and for accountability, you never room alone. All this was new to me. Not only did we share a room, but Guy was another godly example to me. I watched him in amazement as he would open up his Bible every night before bed and read and study for an hour. He would pray by the side of his bed, then call his wife on the phone and carry on a conversation like I'd never heard a husband and wife share. Before he would hang up the phone he would pray for his wife. I was in a place that was very different—somewhat surreal—but somewhere that God wanted me to be.

What was expected of me that first week was more than I'd anticipated, but I did everything I was asked and did it to the best of my ability. Jeff asked me to share my testimony on stage in front of the entire crowd on the second night. They told me to take between five and seven minutes and just share from my heart how I came to know Jesus and what events led me to that decision in my life.

I'd really never done this before but wrote my entire salvation experience down on paper, reviewed it a few times and then shared it with my roommate, Guy. I knew it would be very difficult for me to share in front of a big crowd, whether I knew them or not. I didn't want to be emotional as I shared the most important decision of my life but found it difficult, to say the least, to fight back the tears as I went through my experience from start to finish. It was evident that what I was saying was real and very close to my heart as I had to stop and compose myself a number of times before I could continue. I made it through the five minutes and was complimented by all the guys when I finished. More rewarding was the feedback after the program, when so many people came up to me and told me how my testimony had touched them and had a big part in them coming forward and accepting Christ into their own life. Does it get any better than that? God allowed me to be used to bring another person to Him. Wow!

SNAPPING DOUBLE BATS FOR JESUS

VICTIM OF THE ARM SANDWICH

12
CHAPTER

FEATS OF STRENGTH

THE SPEAKING WAS WHAT MADE ME the most nervous and pushed me out of my comfort zone. But there was much more to Team Impact and what they did to attract a crowd and get people's attention. They did this with feats of strength. This I had no idea how to do. Breaking baseball bats over your leg, blowing up hot water bottles until they exploded in your face, and tearing 2,000-page phone books down the middle like one piece of paper are things one doesn't practice at home.

I was asked the first night to lift a huge, 300-pound tree trunk over my head after it had two notches cut into it for handles, and blow up a hot water bottle until it exploded. I was also asked to drive my arm through a three foot stack of concrete bricks and snap a wooden bat over my leg. This is something these guys did every week!

I got a few tips on form and how to use my strength then I was sent out on stage to perform these unreal tasks in front of hundreds of people. Yeah, no pressure at all! I do believe God's anointing was with me as I was successful at each feat I performed that week.

I had a number of other feats I was asked to perform that week: breaking two baseball bats at one time over my leg, bending a half-inch steel bar in a double loop as I gripped it with my teeth, and having an 800-pound block of ice broken off my chest by a sledge hammer as I was sandwiched between two beds of 1,000 sharp nails.

It only took one week around these guys and experiencing how God could use someone like me doing some of the silliest things you can imagine to win souls to Jesus and I was sold—completely sold. This was what I was called to do, this was where I belonged, this is where God wanted me. A part of my life started to come into perspective. I was given a glimpse of stardom and limelight, but just to use as a stepping-stone to win souls to Jesus. I was still on stage and this time able to be myself, showcase my God-given gifts and use them to glorify Christ. It couldn't get any better than this.

As I traveled from town to town, state to state, and country to country, a number of people who knew me from the WWE and the UFC now saw me as an everyday guy that loved the Lord and wanted to share that love with them. Most people see Christians as weak, frail guys who can't stand up for themselves. This idea of big, professional athletes talking unashamedly about their relationship with Jesus opened the eyes of so many who just came to see a show.

One of the greatest things about Team Impact is the crowd we would draw was not a typical Christian crowd. Most in attendance saw us on a flier, in a gym, or listened to their kids tell them about the strong men that were in school that day. They came to see big, strong guys do unusual feats of strength and went home with a newborn relationship with Jesus Christ. The feats are fun and entertaining, but the decision to invite Jesus into your life is a decision that changes not only your life but your eternity.

13

CHAPTER

HOT WATER BOTTLES

I can't help but see some of my teammates on TI after missing a concrete break and the look of disgust on their faces, but still putting on a smile for the crowd. We all know the pain inside; although it's really not a big deal, we all miss breaks all the time and it actually gives credibility to the feats we do. Regardless, we still don't like to fail at anything and the competitive nature in all of us in unavoidable. It doesn't help that after a miss, the team is pretty unforgiving and the rest of the boys rub it in for the rest of the week. Some newcomers who do some boasting about how good they are or how they never miss really hear it after a missed break or hot water bottle that gets away from them.

The first trip I ever took with Team Impact I was broken in quickly and given many of the more difficult feats of strength to perform right away. There were two reasons for this: (1) to see if I could do them, and (2) to see if I would. We still do this today with new team members to see if they really have what it takes to make it. The physical part of what we do isn't easy. I have seen many who just can't do some of the required physical feats of strength day after day and week after week, and I must admit that blowing up 10-15 hot water bottles in a week is not easy. If you were to ask any of the 17 athletes on our team what the most dreaded feat of strength is on our team, it's the hot water bottle. You just don't know how tiresome one is until you've tried it. I really don't recommend it for anyone, as it can be dangerous. I have had bottles take 75 big breaths before they explode—and when they explode, they explode violently. The rubber from the bottle often wraps back around and slaps you on the face hard enough to leave a large welt, sometimes even cutting the skin. A few team members have lost their hearing for a period because the bottle hit them on the ear so hard. We always wear protective glasses so we don't lose an eye. We always ask the crowd if they know what the hot water bottle is and hold it up high. Most say it's a whoopee cushion. They do resemble whoopee cushions, and the younger generation really has no clue about hot water bottles. They have, for the most part, become a thing of the past with all our new technology in pain relief. If you've never seen a hot water bottle, I urge you to ask your grandparents if they have one. Some drugstores still carry them but they aren't around like they used to be. They're made out of a thick rubber, much denser than any balloon you have ever attempted to blow up.

We often tell our audiences about the hot water bottle and why we do them as a feat of strength. They used to use it on the Wide World of Sports as a feat of strength for the strong men competitors to attempt. Some could do it, some couldn't. But the feat didn't last long because an athlete ended up getting seriously injured from attempting it. I understand he was close to making the bottle explode when something happened and the air from the bottle rushed back inside his lungs, rupturing one of them. It probably happened from pure exhaustion. After that incident the hot water bottles have been banned from strong man competitions.

On our team, it's humorous to see a new guy come on to the team and the first thing we do is hand him a hot water bottle and say, "Here you go, buddy." I know that's just wrong, but it really is a way to see how mentally strong a person is because you really do want to stop before the bottle explodes. On our team we usually take turns doing bottles at schools and night events unless there is a new guy and he isn't doing any speaking yet. New team members really do get broken in mentally and physically. It made me want to be a speaker much sooner, so I learned how to perform a school assembly and developed my testimony as soon as possible.

The members on our team are not there to see anyone embarrassed and definitely not hurt, so we offer all the advice possible on small techniques we've learned over the years to make things easier. The coach in me always enjoys giving helpful tips to my teammates on all the feats of strength we perform. I've witnessed so many athletes in other occupations who are scared for their own jobs or just not good people who don't want to offer advice to help out someone else. What a selfish way to go through life, just taking care of yourself. I believe God honors people who are helpful to others. I can't help but think about the wristband that was so popular a few years back—WWJD (What Would Jesus Do?). I try to think about this in every situation during the day.

14

CHAPTER

ON THE ROAD AGAIN

I LET THE OFFICE KNOW I WAS WILLING TO WORK and travel whenever they needed me. I wanted to be a full-time evangelist. I understood the commitment it would take, the biggest being time on the road. Jeff Neal told me from the start that when you're called into ministry, your wife must also be called because it's a sacrifice that affects the entire family. I was coming out of a career in the WWE where I was gone from my family much more than I was home, so doing a crusade every other week seemed like an easy task at the time.

My wife was excited about the position but still not sold on it like I was. She hadn't met the guys on this team and had no idea what they were all about. The morals and ethics and love for the Lord were something she couldn't grasp by just listening to my stories about what I'd experienced. This was a new world to me also. I'd never been around a team of athletes who were sold out to Jesus, accountable to one another, and modeled a Christian lifestyle like I had never witnessed in my life.

There were over 20 athletes on this team but I'd met only a handful. Each week you go out with a different team and usually a new team leader who's in charge of the crusade for the week. It worked out great—that way the guys could rotate weeks on and off to give them time to spend with their families. The team worked on a schedule similar to the school calendar year.

We depended on school assemblies during the day where we would share a secular message and then invite all the students out to the night crusade where we could share Jesus. The only time we were able to give a testimony in a school or give a message of salvation was in a Christian school. We would get them occasionally. Working around the school calendar, we would have times during the year where we'd be extremely busy and have three or four crusades in one week. So the office would have to schedule four separate teams and coordinate the difficult schedules every month. Ideally, each athlete would work two weeks out of the month and have every other week off, but that wasn't always the case. Putting this schedule together was a task, and pleasing everyone was next to impossible.

Coming out of a very lucrative job with the WWE, I was accustomed to making good money and, well, ministry is not a lucrative position for most. So when I had the opportunity to work extra weeks I would always take them.

Saying *no* has always been difficult for me in almost every situation. When it came to my new job and making a good first impression, it was even more difficult. I don't believe anyone in the office wanted to take advantage of me but there was more than one time I worked six weeks straight. I would fly out Tuesday night and get home Monday morning, wash my clothes, put them back in my suitcase, and head out for another six days. I would justify my time away by saying we needed the money but not really being aware of either my selfishness or the price I was paying to be gone.

The team was good about flying out your wife to be at a crusade with you if you had more than two weeks in a row on the road.

There were a couple times I was able to bring Jody with me and that made a huge impact on my new career and time away. She was able to see the guys I spent my nights away with, not only seeing who they were but what we did night after night. The sacrifice she had to make week after week, not having her husband at home, seemed a little different now. She sat in the crowd and listened to the guys share their stories and at the end of the night, make that call for the lost. As families and children, moms and dads, grandmas and grandpas came walking down that aisle at the end of the night to give their lives to Jesus, the sacrifices seemed like nothing.

15

SCHOOLS

As a new guy on the team, my participation in school assemblies was minimal. I would blow up a hot water bottle, break a bat, bend a steel bar in my teeth, and tear a phone book in half. I would do the build-up on the microphone and tell the students about the night program, explaining that the feats of strength they just witnessed were nothing compared to those they would see then. It was very much a true statement. Concrete, ice, fire, and telephone poles were all feats done only at night at the church. This was the extent of my job at a school assembly.

Although it was just not a lot of fun to blow up a hot water bottle until it exploded in your face, I felt guilty for not doing my part. I needed to learn this presentation and learn it fast. After all, I was a high school teacher. It should be easy for me to get a good presentation of my own, right?

Each athlete had their own specific style of assembly and had a personal story that helped them relate to the kids. Elementary schools obviously required a much different message than high schools, so each athlete had a program for each grade level.

After traveling for a few months with several different team leaders, I had the opportunity to hear many different assemblies and ways to present a powerful message to the kids. Although there were several different messages, each seemed to get the students' attention like I had never before witnessed. As a high school teacher, I had the opportunity to sit in on many different assemblies and motivational speakers. I do remember a few that caught my attention, but never did any have the impact on an entire student body like this.

I began to develop my own style and thought about my own story. What could I possibly tell these students that would help them relate to their life and the struggles they may be facing? It was simple. I didn't have to think very hard since my time in school was anything but a cake walk. It was a battle. I began to write it out on paper, and the more I remembered, the easier it was for me to share that part of my life and my experience with the kids. It turned out that many students are in the very shoes I was as a young kid, and my story relates to more than a few. My elementary school talk was the first I came up with and was comfortable to share. Regardless of the age of students I spoke to, I wanted them to know my message was not to get them to be a world-class athlete but a world-class person.

16

CHAPTER

CHUBBY

AFTER I SHARED MY STORY FOR THE FIRST TIME, I received some great advice from my friend Jeff Neal once again. Jeff is the master of storytelling and can get me on the edge of my seat even today, although I've heard the story he tells a hundred times. So, when Jeff offered me advice I took it. He had me revamp the story to keep it suspenseful, letting the kids guess who I was talking about after the story had already been told. After sharing my story about *Chubby* hundreds and hundreds of times, I have never had a school not guess who Chubby was. Here's how it goes:

Chubby was a big kid. When Chubby was born he weighed over ten pounds. By the time Chubby was in kindergarten he was just about as wide as he was tall. That made Chubby an easy target. He didn't look like the rest of the kids and he got picked on every day.

Chubby not only looked different than the rest of the kids, he struggled in school. Not because he was a bad kid or got in trouble a lot, Chubby just didn't learn as fast as the rest of the kids in his class. As the class turned page after page in their books, Chubby would be stuck on the first. The bell would finally ring for recess and Chubby would take off for the door, but was usually stopped and told he had to stay in and review everything that had been learned that day.

You see, it took Chubby three or four times hearing the same information most kids understood the first time for it to sink in. Chubby would usually end up frustrated, wondering to himself what was wrong with him, why was it that he had to work so much harder and spend so much more time than the rest of the kids, and he still didn't do as well.

Every once in a while Chubby was allowed to go out for recess with the class and, like most schools, the kids would always play games. Two captains jump out to select, one after the other, the kids who got to be on their team. Every time the same thing—when it came down to Chubby, no one wanted him on their team. You see, he wasn't very fast, and couldn't run, kick, catch or throw a ball very well.

Do you know what happens when someone gets picked last every day, who's the kid no one wants on their team? Well, they don't feel very good about themselves. Chubby would often go home upset, wondering why he was different, why he had to work so hard and just couldn't get it. Chubby had very supportive parents who encouraged and praised him every day just to do his best. But that didn't always help the situations at school. First grade, second grade, third grade—all the same day after day—Chubby would take the teasing, sometimes even from the girls in class.

Fourth grade was a turning point in Chubby's life. You see, in the fourth grade Chubby had a teacher he really liked, and of all classes, it was his gym class. Now, Chubby was not very good in gym class. As a matter of fact, he couldn't even make it one lap around the gym floor. He would have to stop and walk. He couldn't do one sit-up and not even one pushup. The kids would jump rope and Chubby would just get all tangled up when he tried.

Despite all the trouble he had in his PE class, Chubby knew his teacher would have a positive comment for him. Not a single class would go by without Chubby's teacher telling him how proud of him he was and that every day Chubby came to PE he was getting a little better, and that he was working very hard. He was told every day to keep up the great work. Chubby wasn't used to hearing these positive things from anyone, so he looked forward to PE class because he knew he would hear something nice from his teacher.

One day Chubby was called over to the side by his gym teacher, not knowing what he was about to hear. Chubby's teacher asked him to try out for the school's wrestling team. Chubby about fell over as he looked up into his teacher's eyes. He said, "You have to be kidding me. I've seen what those guys do—they run around the gym, and climb the rope all the way up to the ceiling, they do pushups and sit-ups, they do pull-ups and, well, I can't do any of those things." But this was Chubby's favorite teacher and Chubby didn't want to let his favorite teacher down, so he said, "I'll try."

At 3:00 that day, the bell rang and Chubby headed straight to the gym. By the end of that week Chubby had never been so tired and sore in his whole life. But you know, by the end of the first week Chubby was able to do a pushup all on his own, a sit-up all by himself, and he made it one full time around the gym floor without stopping and walking!

Another week went by and Chubby did two pushups, two sit-ups, and made it twice around the gym floor without stopping and walking. Another week went by and Chubby found something out. He found out he was a pretty good wrestler. You see, Chubby was short and had a really low center of gravity so when his opponent would shoot in and grab his leg—forget it.

Chubby wasn't going anywhere and if he fell on you, you were squished!

One more week passed and the team began to compete against other schools and Chubby began to win. All of a sudden, the kids who made fun of Chubby were running up to him patting him on the back and telling him what a great job he had done. Chubby was amazed, not knowing what to do or how to act, but liked the way winning made him feel. He liked it so much that he worked even harder to be the best he could be. He would do pushups and sit-ups on his own, and give all he had day after day in practice. By the end of the season Chubby had become one of the best wrestlers on the team.

Chubby liked this so much he wrestled again as a fifth grader, a sixth grader, a seventh grader...and by the time Chubby was in his last year of school they didn't call him Chubby any more. He had worked so hard, spent so much time being the best wrestler he could be that he had become the biggest, strongest kid in the whole school, and one of the best wrestlers in the State of Colorado.

Chubby had spent so much time with his teachers, often getting extra help before and after school, and he had spent so much time with his coaches, working himself to exhaustion night after night, that Chubby had earned himself a scholarship to a university. Just as most young kids have a dream of who they want to be and what they want to do when they grow up, Chubby had one as well. You see, Chubby had spent so much time with his teachers and coaches as he went through school that it made a lifelong impact on him. Chubby wanted to be a teacher and coach so he could go back into schools and help those kids just like he'd been—kids who wanted to do well but had a difficult time learning and keeping up with the rest of the kids.

Five years later Chubby graduated from college as one of the best wrestlers in the nation and earned a degree to be a high school teacher and coach. Chubby became a high school teacher and coach, but didn't want to stop there. He wanted to be the best teacher and coach he could be, so he went back to school two years later and earned a masters degree.

Chubby had a lot of physical goals in his life, so he continued to work and train every day. After coaching and teaching for nine years, Chubby was flown to Stamford, Connecticut and met the McMahons of the WWE. Chubby was offered a four year developmental contract to compete in the WWE. Nine months later, Chubby was in Madison Square Garden, wrestling against some of the biggest names in the WWE, in front of 20,000 screaming fans.

A few years later, Chubby had the best opportunity of all. He was able to travel around the world and speak to thousands of students every week about their dreams and goals and some important decisions they would have to make for those dreams to come true.

I always end my story by asking the kids if they know who Chubby is, and they always guess it right. Chubby was me. I was the short, fat, little kid who got picked on all the way to the fourth grade. I ask the kids if they understand what the story is all about. It doesn't matter where you start the race, it's where you finish that counts.

There were so many times that I went home from school and told my parents *I give up, forget it, I quit.* But I had parents who supported me and teachers that never gave up. I made a choice at a young age that I was going to hang around friends who would be there to support me and pat me on the back in hard times, not ones who would ask me to jeopardize my values and get me to do things I knew were wrong. I needed to stay away from "friends" who would keep me from reaching my dreams and goals for my life. One thing I've realized about friends who make poor choices is that misery loves company.

17

CHAPTER

PEER PRESSURE

WHEN I STEP INTO MOST MIDDLE and senior high schools, it's evident that many of the kids have already joined a peer group. Each group—athletes, scholars, band students, thespians, or rebels—has specific clothing, hairstyles, and attitudes that set it apart from the others.

Several of the schools I've visited were hardcore. In some inner city schools, outsiders wouldn't even consider holding an hour-long presentation in front of a thousand students. However, some of the roughest schools I've spoken in had crowds that listened the best. They knew what I had to say was for their benefit and that I was sincere.

Whether I was at a Christian school or not, God's anointing was over me every time. I might have felt so uneasy and worried that I would never get the kids' attention, but the minute I took the microphone and began to speak, I could feel the anointing come over me. I got such a feeling of comfort that I was able to look out and see the kids' eyes focused on me and what I was about to share.

I am straightforward about peer pressure and trying to fit in with the crowd. In those situations, we end up saying and doing things we normally wouldn't, just to fit in. My message is simple: *If you have to do or say something that jeopardizes your morals, standards, beliefs, or character just to be accepted by a group, you don't need those people in your life. It's better to stand up for what you know is right, even when it means being alone.*

The program *60 Minutes* ran a documentary about slaughter houses and how one in particular solved their delay problem. The sheep in a large pen had to go down a series of three chutes. At the end of the third chute the sheep would be put to death. The problem was that they couldn't get the sheep to feed into the chutes; they would just mill around aimlessly.

The owners finally found a man who said he could solve the problem. He brought a goat and put it in the pen. The man sat on the fence and blew his whistle once. The goat ran along the perimeter of the pen. After five minutes a good number of sheep began to do laps around the pen behind the goat. Ten minutes later, all 500 sheep formed a perfect line behind the goat. The goat trainer blew his whistle twice. The goat headed for the first shoot. He went down 100 yards and took a left, went down 100 more and took a right, then went the last 50 yards. At the end, they opened the gate and let the goat slip out. They shut the gate and slaughtered the sheep, one by one.

As I watched this program, I realized that many of our youth are no different than the sheep. So many follow someone who claims to be their friend, yet is leading them to their destruction. Misery loves company and when someone does something wrong, it's easier to deal with when their friends are doing it alongside them. It's often those we call our "friends" who talk us into taking that first drink, or puffing on that first cigarette, or doing something worse.

Sometimes we need to step back and look at who we're spending the majority of our time with. Are they asking us to do things that go against our morals, character, and beliefs? If so, it's time we stand up for what we know is right, even if we have to stand alone and find new friends. It sounds easy, but it's a very hard thing to do. Some of our friends have good qualities in addition to the bad, but in the long run we will be glad we made the decision to stick to our morals.

18

CHAPTER

TRAVEL

As traveling became more consistent it became harder to be away from my family. I wondered what life would be like again not living out of a suitcase. I remembered the words of Mark 1:17: *"Come, follow me," Jesus said, "and I will make you fishers of men."* The weeks began to roll together and at the end of the month I couldn't even tell you the towns I had just been in.

Christ would always be faithful week after week, as He would anoint me in every way possible. When I was down physically, He would give me strength to perform my feats of strength. If I was emotionally drained, He would put a smile on my face and the energy to comfort others in need. When I needed a spiritual lift, the Lord would bring someone who would bless me beyond measure and usually in an unexpected way. Sometimes it would be someone who let me know the impact my testimony had on them. Knowing that the Lord is using you to bring others to Him is the greatest feeling one can achieve.

Our schedules would be similar week after week. Fly into a new town, get picked up by the church van and make small talk all the way back to the church. Sometimes that ride would be two or three hours, depending on how small of a town we were traveling to. Oftentimes we would get picked up by the youth pastor, associate pastor, or just a member of the church. We would get an idea of what to expect for the week, the size of the church, how many school assemblies we would be doing, the hotel and gym arrangements, and how hard the church had worked organizing the event. It was usually all pretty evident by the time we reached the church what to expect from the week. One thing we didn't know was all the souls that God was going to use us to reach in that community. Every night I would be astonished by how God could move and how He could use the strange things of the world to save the lost. It was usually in the roughest places that God used us the most, a town where during the message kids would be crying and running up and down the aisles. Adults would seem to be disengaged from the message, and the microphone would cut out every other word. This is when the Lord would remind us who is always in control and that it wasn't us. It was nights like this that Jesus would bring forward an entire family weeping uncontrollably or the town's drug dealer or an elderly person who couldn't make it up the aisle without a walker.

There was one thing that never grew old, regardless of how many times it happened—salvation. Seeing one or hundreds walk forward and give their life to Christ gave me goose bumps. Every night, it was as if it was the first time I had seen it happen. It was a divine appointment for all those who were in attendance, but we had no control over it.

We would ask for another commitment from those who made decisions for Jesus: A commitment to stand for Jesus and walk to the front of the altar where we could pray over the best decision they'd ever made. For most, it's easy to slip up a hand when everyone's head is bowed and eyes are closed. It's a different story to stand up in front of a town that knows who you are, what you've done, and where you've been. Some had gone to church for years but never gave their life to Christ. They fear what everyone will say when they stand up and walk forward. Others simply have too much pride to get up and make the walk to the front of the room.

When I would make the count to three and have them come forward, the kids would immediately jump up and run to the altar. In Matthew 19:14, Jesus said, "Let the little children come to me, and do not hinder them, for the kingdom of heaven belongs to such as these."

The adults would begin to look around for others to commit before they did. Before I asked them to make their public profession of faith, I let them know what the Bible says in Mark 8:38: "If anyone is ashamed of me and my words in this adulterous and sinful generation, the Son of Man will be ashamed of him when he comes in his Father's glory with the holy angels."

19
CHAPTER

THE WALK

IF YOU CAN'T TAKE 20 STEPS TO THE ALTAR in a church where people will applaud and celebrate the greatest decision you ever made, then what makes you think you will last 20 seconds in the real world where people will persecute you for your belief in Jesus Christ? I tell them about my salvation experience: I was in my hometown in front of everyone who knew me, everyone who knew where I had been and what I had done. But when it was time to make the walk to the altar, to make a public profession of the decision I had just made, I was the first one out of my seat and to the front. I left my pride right back in my seat where it belonged.

What some people don't understand is that this is the victory lap. It is like the track and field athlete who, after winning the gold medal, grabs his country's flag, pulls it across his back, and takes a slow lap around the stadium while the spectators cheer at the top of their lungs. This is the time to stand and take the victory walk to the altar and receive the greatest medal ever— the gift of salvation and eternal life.

Week after amazing week I would see adults—moms and dads—raise their hands to accept Christ into their life. They would say the sinner's prayer, but when the time came to stand and walk to the front of the room they would forget the prayer they just said. I would make direct eye contact with some and give them a little nod letting them know I saw their hand and that it was okay to come forward, but most of the time it was met with a blank stare. It's not the walk that saves them but the prayer to ask Christ into their heart, but staying in their seat and keeping this great decision to themselves gives Satan a grip and some ammunition to start to convince them that maybe it wasn't real.

It's always enjoyable to watch the children, as they have no problem getting out of their chairs and running right up to the front, sometimes even jumping right up on the stage to stand next to me. But it's the teenagers and adults who really move me when I see the sincerity of the decision, when I see them crying from the confession of their sin and finally surrendering to God's grace. Oftentimes it's hard for me to hold back my emotion regardless of how many times I have witnessed salvations.

20

CHAPTER

DOUBLE DUTY

TRAVEL WAS STEADY WITH TEAM IMPACT, although I still had aspirations of making extra money and climbing the ranks in MMA. I joined TI right after my WWE career had ended, so going back to MMA seemed a logical thing to do. I never really wanted to commit myself to doing MMA fulltime, mainly because at the time there weren't very many fighters actually making a good living from it. So, as I began my new career with Team Impact, I would take fights. When I first started back, most of them were in Japan. It was a fun experience to travel to Japan and fight in front of a completely different crowd than what I had been used to in the USA, especially coming out of the WWE.

I'll never forget my first fight after my three-year stint in the WWE. My manager, Phyllis Lee, booked me in Pancrase, one of the oldest but most stable fighting organizations in the world. I was to face off against a well-known Japanese fighter by the name of Kengo Watanabe He was very big for a Japanese fighter and had come off a couple wins before I was matched up with him.

I was amazed at how small everything in Japan was, from the people to hotel rooms to the meals. I felt like a giant.

I was treated with much respect from the Japanese fans, fighters, and promoters from the very start. They are so much more organized and structured than we are here in the States. I was handed my itinerary as soon as I stepped off the plane, given an envelope with meal money, and had an interpreter by my side in case I needed anything. The 13-hour flight was a little exhausting, but it would be the last time I flew coach for that trip. My brother went with me on this trip as my corner, along with Phyllis Lee. She was on all my Japan trips as she was respected in Japan even more than I was. She had been booking fighters and pro wrestlers over there for years and had made that trip many times.

My first Pancrase fight would be the main event of the evening as they had built Kengo up to be the next big Japanese star. He had been a stand-out soccer player in Japan prior to his fighting career, so he was already well-known to Japanese fans. I was a bit nervous since it was my first fight in over three years. I had begun to travel with Team Impact, so my training was not as good as it could have been because I was working full time and on the road constantly. I had little to worry about. I took Kengo out in under two minutes of the first round with a key lock that dislocated his elbow. It was on tight and he just wouldn't tap so something had to give.

I returned to Japan consistently over the next three years with Pancrase, Pride fighting championships, and New Japan Pro Wrestling. For most of my Japan fights, I had Team Impact teammates travel with me and corner me. It's a neat experience for someone who has never traveled to Japan plus the excitement of actually cornering a friend in this environment. Many of my teammates were able to stand in my corner. Most of my Japan fights were over quickly; only two went the distance so it was easy work for them.

21

CHAPTER

HOUSTON, TEXAS

IN HOUSTON, I STOOD IN ONE OF THE CHURCH ROOMS with a big, black shiner from an MMA fight the week before. Dr. Ed Young came to pray with us before we went on stage. He said something to us that night that really hit home and has stuck with me to this day. He said, "Tonight I want you to go out and preach and perform like it was your first night."

Traveling as much as we did, it was easy to get into a routine and go through the motions to some extent. Breaking huge walls of burning concrete and lifting telephone poles over your head shouldn't seem routine, but it was to us. The feats of strength were the easy parts, the no-brainers. If anything was going to be routine, that's what you would want to be routine.

When we preached the Word of God it was always anointed. I can't tell you how many times I shared my testimony over the years, and even many of the same stories I used to tie-in to a salvation message. Each time it was like the first, yet a little different, in a new place with a new crowd and ears that needed to hear what I was sharing. The Lord would night after night give me such blessings, and the people in attendance would comment on the impact of the word I shared and how it affected them. The greatest compliment one could give me was letting me know it was something the Lord gave me to share that directly influenced them to give their life to Jesus.

It was in Houston that the team set a record for the number of school assemblies we performed in one week. We had about every member of the team on this crusade because of the schools. We ended up with 126 school assemblies with five teams of two guys doing four or five assemblies a day. Often we would even have to split up and do school programs solo. That worked okay if it was an elementary school, but having to do high schools alone was not a lot of fun.

The staff at Second Baptist was one of the finest I ever had the pleasure of working with. I still stay in contact with a few of them. Becky, Leti, and Lauren were three of the youth leaders who worked hard that week organizing, scheduling, and getting the team from one school to the next. It ran like clockwork, for the most part.

Second Baptist had three campuses, so we would split up at night into three groups and do our program in three locations at once. It was a great success, as the shows were full to capacity night after night. After five school assemblies and a bigger than normal night event, we were ready for a good night's rest. The physical stress was one thing,, but the mental fatigue of speaking that much was draining beyond belief.

The number of salvations for the week was well worth the hard work and effort to make it happen. To this day, I haven't spoken to any schools as rough as some of those in inner city Houston. But as I said before, the Lord has a way of calming even the roughest of schools when He puts someone in there to do His work. It was in some of those schools that I feel like I was being used the most and had an audience that God wanted to get hold of. Night after night, we saw some of these kids walking up the aisle at the end of the night with tears in their eyes, giving their life over to Christ and taking a new direction. How can anyone ever get tired of seeing this? So when Dr. Young told us to "perform like it was our first time," he could have saved his breath, because to us every night was a first night!

**CHUCK LIDDELL AND I IN JAPAN
FOR THE PRIDE FIGHTING CHAMPIONSHIPS**

KEVIN RANDLEMAN AND I BEFORE A PRIDE EVENT

22

CHAPTER

HOMETOWN CRUSADE

I'LL NEVER FORGET MY FIRST CRUSADE at my home church in Greeley, Colorado. I hadn't been with the team for very long and had my pastor set up the crusade. It was really a great experience to bring the team into the Greeley Wesleyan Church. It was amazing to have the opportunity to tell people I knew and many I grew up with about Jesus and to show what Christ had done in my life and how he had totally transformed me.

My boys were able to see firsthand what their dad did when he was gone from home. The boys helped me prepare the stage every night, which took about an hour. Cutting ice, stacking concrete, and setting up breaks was not an easy task and usually took 10 to 15 stage hands in addition to the team to get everything ready to go.

I had a lot of pressure on me during the week, having organized most of the school assemblies and making sure everything went smoothly. I wanted my church to be impressed by the team and what we were all about. Night after night the crowds grew larger and larger and the last two nights the church actually had to turn people away. They had filled up the overflow rooms and put people everywhere possible.

I was able to share my testimony a couple times during the week which was a little scary because of the amount of people at the programs who knew my past life, where I had been, and what I had done. My testimony was more relevant than ever; after all, I was saved right there in that church. When I spoke of the time that I accepted Christ into my life, I could point to the seat I was in when I made that decision. It was powerful, so real, and so emotional.

The Lord used me and the other members that night in a great way and at the end of the night I was brought to my knees once again. Jeff Neal shared a message and extended the invitation to ask Christ into their lives. During this time, I always go into a deep prayer asking Jesus to move and for everyone to open their hearts and really feel the presence of the Lord. Jeff had everyone close their eyes and try to remember the time they asked Christ into their life.

The Bible says in John 3:3, "*That unless a man is born again he is not fit for the kingdom of God.*" So many think they can just be good enough to enter heaven, but that's not the case. There must be a time in your life that you ask Jesus to be your Savior.

When Jeff asked this question, I prayed and looked around the room as hand after hand rose in the air to accept Christ. What hit me hard was that my own brother put his hand in the air, and sitting next to him were my mother, and my sister, both with their hands up high. I could hardly contain my emotion. Next Jeff asked them to walk forward and make a public profession of their faith. All three walked forward and I made my way through the crowd, put my arms around them, and couldn't hold back the tears of joy any longer. Wow, what a night! It just doesn't get any better than that.

23

CHAPTER

HOMETOWN FIGHT

ON TOP OF THE PRESSURE OF THE WEEK with this crusade, I had even more stress looming over me. I had an MMA fight that Saturday night. I had to miss the last night of the crusade to compete at the Pepsi Center in front of a Colorado crowd I hadn't fought in front of for years. I trained as much as I possibly could before the fight, but Team Impact had me very busy.

For two weeks before this I had been out of the country in Haiti doing a crusade with Larry Jones and "Feed the Children." Haiti was not a great place to travel to and prepare for an MMA fight. It was by far the most eye-opening place I had ever encountered. The degree of poverty can't be imagined by most. I often remember that time when I think I have it bad. The living conditions were beyond belief and the things these people had to do every day to survive were unimaginable.

We stayed in one of the nicest hotels on the island but were instructed not to drink the water or eat anything that was even washed in the water there. We also had to be careful where we went, as Haiti was not a safe place to wander around. There were many stories of riots breaking out and people getting shot—you just didn't go to certain parts of town.

It was one of the first times in my life I really felt like a disciple for Christ, risking my life to share the Word of God. We went to the bad parts of town and in the streets we would begin to do feats of strength and gather crowds. We would have speakers set up and begin to share a salvation message. Never did I feel at risk or in danger, although the people escorting us around town were nervous.

I had a couple opportunities to train during the week but most of it was on my own. Berry, my teammate for the week, was a college wrestler and 350-pound athlete, so that was a plus. But Berry wasn't in shape to go for very long and couldn't push my cardio endurance like I needed him to. So I swam laps early every morning before our day began. I would go out to the pool and swim 50 laps as fast as I could go.

I was advised not to go running in the streets and don't know if it would have been possible anyway. The streets were unreal— huge pot holes, trash everywhere, and no toilets, so people would just go in the streets and didn't really care who saw them.

The Crusade was a big success as we filled the National Stadium the last night with thousands of people. It was raining hard outside but we went on with the show. Barry and I opened up the night with feats of strength then a testimony from me and a story from Berry. Larry Jones finished up the night with an amazing salvation message that moved everyone. It was a challenge to speak because we had to stop after every sentence and wait for the translator and it was difficult to keep focused. Hundreds and hundreds came forward that night and accepted Christ.

So coming back home, I was a bit worn out, my stomach a bit upset from the food, and a hometown crusade a couple days out. It's just one of the things I learned to deal with as a fighter—you just do as much as you can to prepare and train as hard as possible. I had a couple opportunities to train the week after I returned. I was with a group of the strongest, best athletes around: Jeff Neal, the former Houston Oiler and power-lifting champion, Siolo Towaeffa, an amazingly strong and talented athlete, and Randall Harris, a Junior Power-lifting Gold Medalist—all well over 300 pounds and all came in on me one at a time over and over and over. I would go for an hour to an hour and a half straight, staying in the middle the whole time with no breaks. It gave the rest of the team the amount of cardio it takes to compete in MMA. It doesn't matter how big or strong or talented you are if you can't breathe. I think that was the biggest eye opener to most guys I trained with—the endurance it takes.

I was the main event fight of the night, so the guys were able to finish the show that Saturday night and still make it from Greeley to Denver in time to walk out with me for my fight and corner me. My friends and family were there that night along with thousands of people in my home state.

This IFC "Global Domination" card featured some of today's biggest MMA stars: Jeremy Horn, Nate Marquardt, Forrest Griffin, Shogun Rua, and my opponent Jerry Verbonic, a 295-pound brawler known as "Scary Jerry." He was a stand-in fighter for Joe "Diesel" Riggs, who backed out of the fight a couple weeks prior.

The fight didn't go like I had planned as Jerry held his own for two rounds. I took him to the mat right away and controlled him on the ground, looking for submission attempts. I was surprised at his strength and ability to fight out of numerous key locks and arm bars. The third round was no different as I took the fight to the ground, but the Colorado altitude was taking a toll on my lungs. I finally locked up an arm bar and cranked it with all I had left. Jerry tapped before his shoulder dislocated and I won again by a tap-out submission. Considering the amount of preparation I had for this event, I was blessed to come out of it with a victory. I was also very glad that my opponent was not seriously injured as well.

It bothers me to hear fighters today who want to physically hurt their opponents. I don't believe that's what this sport is about. Competition and a strong desire to win is one thing, but there is no place for wishing physical or permanent harm to your opponent.

24

CHAPTER

MY BROTHER

It was really a blessing to have my Team Impact brothers in my corner that night, helping me prepare, coaching and praying over me. My brother, Harry, was also in my corner helping coach me to victory. He had cornered me several times and even made the trip to Japan to corner me in my first Pancrase event. Growing up with Harry and wrestling with him my whole life made him a great coach and motivator for me. He knows me well and usually knows what I'm thinking before I do.

Preparing for my first UFC fight, I tried to round up as many athletes as I could, sometimes just big, strong athletes: football players, former wrestling partners, lifters from the gym, and, of course, any martial artists who were willing to join.

This was the late 90s, so MMA training camps were not real popular yet. Most fighters just trained in the field they were experienced in. Boxers boxed and wrestlers wrestled, martial artists went to the dojo and practiced their particular form of martial arts. This particular Sunday morning, after church, I had a group of guys lined up to train with me at Greeley West High School where I taught and coached.

I would usually stay out in the middle and have each guy rotate in after I had tapped out the one before. Sometimes the guys would stay in for two or three goes, depending on how long it took for me to tap them out. I would usually start on my feet with the more advanced guys and with some I would start on my knees so I didn't hurt them with a hard takedown or slam.

After an hour of constant live goes with me in the middle, everyone was pretty well drained and ready to call it good. The last rotation I had with my brother I shot in on a double leg and his heel caught on the mat. His knee hyper-extended terribly and popped loud enough for people across the gym to hear it. He fell to the ground in pain and immediately knew his knee was blown out. We managed to get him into the backseat of a car and to the emergency room, where we sat and waited for hours, of course, before we were helped.

It just so happened to be Super Bowl Sunday and we were sitting in an emergency room. I felt about as low as a person could get, knowing I put my own brother out of commission and probably for a long time. After a few tests, X-rays and MRIs, it was evident that Harry not only tore his Meniscus, but his ACL as well. Both were completely blown out. He had to have knee reconstruction done and would be out nine months with rehab to get back to somewhat normal again. My brother was also a teacher and coach and a very active guy himself.

It goes without saying that my brother hasn't done much training with me since that day, not that he doesn't want to, but he knows he will have to face his wife Kari if anything were to happen again. I would probably have met my match with her so I didn't push that issue. Kari is an amazing woman. I tell her all the time I wish she had a clone. My brother is very blessed to have her. They are one of the most compatible couples I have ever known.

It's hard for me to imagine a greater couple. I have never spoken with anyone who doesn't like them, not that they would tell me if they did. They now have two wonderful children; Payton is two and Calen is four. Kari is a nurse educator and Harry, after being a teacher, athletic director, and assistant principal, is now the Assistant Commissioner for the Colorado High School Activities Association. He had to move an hour away last year for this position in Denver, which has been a bummer, but he loves his job and it's a great fit for him.

25

MY START IN MMA

THE THREE GUYS WHO I CREDIT for talking me into doing my first MMA competition were Greg Becker, a local fireman with a black belt in jujitsu, and a great high school wrestler; Troy Pettyjohn, a tough stand-up fighter with a good ground game; and Curtis, who also worked at Greeley West and was a big, strong grappler. They had convinced me to come and train with them and after I did, I had the itch to take it a step further.

None of the submission attempts worked on me as I powered through them and, being a college wrestler, always stayed in good position and didn't make myself vulnerable. I quickly learned submissions that would work for me as a wrestler. Most of the submissions were just moves that were illegal in wrestling, so most came very naturally.

I also had some pressure from my high school wrestlers who constantly told me I needed to be a UFC fighter. This was at the time when guys like Dan Severn, Mark Kerr, and Mark Coleman were dominating the UFC, beating up on boxers, sumo wrestlers, most martial artists, and barroom brawlers. I would have the team over to my house to watch the UFC events on Pay per View a couple times during the season. The UFC didn't have promotions and air every month like it does now.

Many on the team made the road trip to Denver to watch my first fights at the Bas Rutten Invitational. It was a neat feeling to see their faces light up when they heard I was going to be invited to fight in the next UFC after only one tournament and three quick wins under my belt. The buzz quickly shot around the high school and my small town, where ultimate fighting was pretty much unheard of.

26

CHAPTER

UFC STEREOTYPES

Ultimate fighting in the late 90s was still not a common name like it is today. It wasn't long after I'd been in the sport and was preparing for my first UFC competition that my pastor called me up to the front of the church one Sunday morning and asked me to explain what I was getting ready to do. As I told them a little bit about the sport I could see many shaking their heads in disbelief.

I just smiled and acted like it was just another day at the office. I explained to them that this was just another sport to me, no different than a wrestling match or football game. But I could see many still didn't get it and thought that it should be no part of a Christian man's life.

Pastor Steve Wilson announced that he signed me up to be an usher. He thought if anyone was not going to give in the offering, I would be the one they had to face. They did get a laugh out of that one. He first put me at the front door to be a Sunday morning greeter, but that didn't work out very well either, as everyone kept pulling out their ID's at the door. I had to explain to them, "No, I'm not a bouncer and you can put your ID away, you're old enough to come to church." Although there were a few dress code violations— wow—and at church! God welcomes us all regardless of what we wear and what we look like.

All joking aside, there are still many who don't approve of what I do and think it's still a barbaric sport and something a Christian man just shouldn't be doing. To this day, my mother, who knows me better than just about anyone, gets ill when she knows I have accepted a fight. She can't even watch it on TV and waits by the phone at all hours of the night until she gets a call letting her know I'm okay. She will bribe me with just about anything not to fight. It's not that she isn't supportive, she just can't stand to see me get hit or injured in any way. After I've had 26 professional fights and a few minor injuries, she is still not a fan of MMA. I guess if I had to think of my boys entering a cage for an NHB fight, I wouldn't be real excited either. It's always different when it's your own.

I used to laugh at all the crazy parents when I was a high school wrestling coach. I could pick out the parents of the wrestler on the mat right away. The screaming and body positioning in the stands or on the side of the mat would make them look more than ridiculous. I would always laugh and shake my head in embarrassment for them.

I did that until my own two boys stepped on the mat. I would catch myself doing the same thing, not knowing or caring if anyone was around me. It's amazing what that emotion can do to a person. So when my mom makes a big deal out of me stepping into a steel cage against another fighter as big as I am, I can understand her pain.

Today Ultimate Fighting has become a household name. Just about everyone has watched it at one time or another. Most men can name their favorite UFC fighters and, oddly, many women can, too.

I always had the feeling when I started this sport that it would explode into a mainstream sport and, yes, take over the sport of boxing in time. I'm glad about the progress the sport has made and the direction it's gone. It went from a bit on the barbaric side in 1994 when the sport began in the USA to what it has become today. Athletes now devote their lives and careers to this sport, training eight hours a day, every day of the week. It's not a part-time job for weekend warriors anymore.

When I started the sport, I was teaching high school art classes, coaching football and wrestling, and was 33 years old and married with two sons. Not a typical life situation for someone to start an ultimate fighting career, but as you can see, my life has been anything but typical. It was easy to break into because of the transition from wrestling to grappling, but I still had so much to learn, and shooting right to the UFC octagon didn't give me much time to learn.

Wrestling was a huge contributor to my success as a fighter but I have to credit most of my success to the fact that I never stopped training and staying in great physical shape. I always wondered what God's plan for me was and why I wasn't ever able to achieve the goals I had set out for myself in high school or college wrestling. I think that fact made me continue to strive for more after my college wrestling career was done.

A BLOODY X1 HEAVYWEIGHT CHAMPIONSHIP

27

CHAPTER

MR. COLORADO

I DIDN'T KNOW WHAT PATH TO TAKE but I knew that physically there was something else in store for me down the road. I continued to hit the gym every day and at the end of the year could count on one hand the days I missed working out. Dedication and consistency were traits my parents and coaches had instilled in me over the years.

A year out of college wrestling I hit the bodybuilding stage and won Mr. Northern Colorado. A few years after that I won my division in the Mr. Natural Colorado Bodybuilding Championships, and then placed in the top three in the Natural USA Championships. It was great to be able to say that I did it, but that diet can really take a toll on an athlete's mind and body. I respect what bodybuilders go through to compete and be successful. The gym and training is the easy part—it's the diet and discipline that amaze me.

Looking back, it's amazing how diets change over time. Protein wasn't a big deal. Believe it or not, I was on a pure carbohydrate diet to lose fat, keep my size, and prepare for my contest. I started to diet hard for each competition about three months out. I stayed in good shape and never carried around much fat. Three months was about the right amount of time for me to really focus at the gym and on my diet. I'm one of those people who puts their mind to something and that's it. Dedication and discipline are two qualities I've been blessed with. I wouldn't cheat on my diet or a workout and mapped out my days to the "T."

With the carbohydrate diet, I would count fat grams, not calories. I was down to three grams of fat the week of the show. If you look at just about any wrapper listing carbs, there will be more than three fat grams per serving—most items have more than that in just one bite. Regardless of how silly this diet seems now, it worked. My body transformed in three months down to two and a half percent body fat by the day of the contest. I did hours of cardio work every day and lifted high reps to define and striate my muscles, but ended up losing too much size in the process, I think. I went from 255 pounds to 215 the day of the show.

It was a great experience, but I'm not sure if I would want to put myself through that diet again. Who knows though? I always need a challenge in front of me, so it's not out of the question.

I would crave some foods after depriving myself of them for three months. So, of course, the day after the show I had to eat them all. Boy, did I pay for that. Your body is so pure from eating clean that when you start putting pizza and ice cream and fried food in it, you're going to pay. Well I did, and didn't even make it out of the restaurant. I had to run to the restroom with cold sweats and decide which I would do first: hover over the toilet or sit on it, because both were needed and fast. After my next competition, I told myself I wouldn't make the same mistake again, but I did. I just couldn't refuse the pizza and again paid a dear price for every enjoyable piece I shoved in my mouth.

Over the years, the diet and nutrition have changed greatly, and so have my eating habits. I think as we grow older we start to understand how our bodies react to foods and we realize what we should and should not eat. High protein diets are now much more common than the high carb diets. I don't cut carbohydrates out like I hear many people doing, but I do cut them back, especially late at night.

I continued to gradually put on size and mass year after year of training, eating well, and never getting out of shape or sloppy. I am to this day very concerned about my appearance and want to be a couple months out of competing shape at all time. I get away with eating just about anything I want just because I work out and do enough cardio to burn it off. With an hour of cardio and another of weight training, I burn enough calories each day that a pizza night or a desert now and then doesn't affect me much.

Eating healthy is not dieting a month here and there. It really is a lifestyle and I choose to eat high protein and keep my carbohydrates to a minimum, especially at night. Another big help to me is I eat every three hours, not always a lot, but enough to keep the furnace fueled.

**CELEBRATING A VICTORY
WITH MY MANAGER PHYLLIS LEE**

28

CHAPTER

TRAINING LIFESTYLE

My metabolism stays as high as it should, even as I get older. So many people try to lose weight by cutting out meals and just not eating enough. Their metabolism slows down as their body craves and stores all the fat it can from the nutrients they're putting in. I talk to people all the time who don't eat breakfast and very little for lunch, but they go out and have a huge dinner before bed. That is the worst thing you can do. You're storing all those calories right before bedtime and not burning off any of them. This is when your body converts all the extra carbohydrates to fat.

The scale has never been a good motivator for me—I've always preferred the mirror. Many people drive themselves crazy by stepping on the scale each day and going nuts when it varies. When you start to train you begin to build muscle and, as you know, muscle weighs more than fat, so your weight goes up. You may be losing pounds of fat but the scale doesn't reflect that because of the muscle gain. This is the perfect scenario and what you want to achieve. Look in the mirror and not down at a scale. Most women like to judge their weight gain and loss by the way their clothes fit them. I would prefer even that over the scale.

Big muscles have always intrigued me. Like many males my age, Arnold Schwarzenegger was one of the first bodybuilders I remember. Ever since the first time I saw a picture of him in *Muscle and Fitness* magazine I told myself that's how I want to look. I can't forget the picture of his bicep and then looking down at mine and wondering if I could ever look like that. I believe that moment is what inspired me to train..

I remember it like it was yesterday. I was riding the bus to Brentwood Middle School, looking out the window. It's funny how some things stick in our minds and leave a mark, the same way some songs do. My parents bought my first weight set when I was 12 years old, and that was the beginning. I had big, red, concrete-filled weights and a brown bench with a leg curl attachment. I remember going to the basement and doing my routine day after day. It wasn't long before I saw some results and my friends did, too. It's always a motivator when others see your gains. A small compliment goes a long way.

Most of the looks didn't come from girls but from other boys. It's funny how we can be so consumed with our appearance and spend countless hours in the gym and eat right for years to look our best, yet most women prefer a lean, skinny guy. Looking back at my life, I wasted too much time trying to be big and lean. Sure, it helped me in athletics and in competition, but if I knew then what I do now, I would have changed a lot of things.

29

CHAPTER

ISS

I WAS REALLY BLESSED IN THE WWE to meet a gym owner in Louisville, Kentucky, by the name of Tillman. He was a bodybuilder himself and a great guy. One day he overheard me talking about wanting a supplement sponsor, so he began to help me as a sponsor with Integrated Sports Science (ISS) products. He was a representative for the company and began to give me a good supply of protein, creatine, glutamine, multivitamins, and recovery drinks every month. It ended up being two or three hundred dollars worth every month and at the time was a huge help to me.

Tillman was hooking me up the entire time I was in Louisville with OVW training, but once I was called up to travel and move back home I didn't get in to Powerhouse to get supplies each month. Tillman gave me Kevin DeHaven's phone number, one of the owners of ISS, so I made the call and was added to their list of professional athletes they sponsored. I felt very honored because their number one athlete and poster boy was none other than Jay Cutler, who would become Mr. Olympia a few years later. I am now one of the featured athletes on their website at http://www.issresearch.com/ronwaterman.php.

What a blessing ISS has been in my life over the years. I continue to get a large amount of supplements each month and stay in great health and shape largely because of it. They're great people and I've had the privilege of hanging out with them at Mr. Olympia the last few years. It's hard to get the necessary amount of vitamins and protein every day with diet alone, so supplements have been a key ingredient to my success the last eight years.

As athletes continue to improve, so does the amount of nutrition it takes to advance their bodies. Recovery time, injury prevention, and muscle and cardiovascular growth are just a few of the elements that have come a long way in the last few years, and they continue to advance by leaps and bounds. If you look at athletes today compared to those 20 years ago, you can see the amazing changes in body physiques as well as results in scores, numbers, and records.

30

CHAPTER

THE PAST

How many times have you wanted to go back and change things from the past? I was in a Bible study not long ago and Sylvester, a brother in Christ, told me to never regret my past. He explained that there was a purpose and a lesson in all we've done, and the things we've done in our past—both good and bad—have made us into the person we are today. We've all had a different journey and mine has been so blessed. I could dwell on the hard times and get caught up in the struggles but I choose to remember the blessings and things that the Lord has given me. Wow, who am I to complain about anything, ever?

One of the things I do when I'm having a rough day is find a quiet spot and shut my mind down. I step out of my body and look at my life, my family, my house, all the Lord has given me, and look up. I've been given so much and should be so grateful for all I have, so when I catch myself feeling sorry or sad or discontented, it's turned into shame for allowing myself to think that way.

With Team Impact, I traveled to Haiti and South Africa and saw the poverty, hardship, and living conditions of everyday life—and these Christians were happy and grateful. They worshipped the Lord like I've never seen. Who I am I to allow myself to feel sad for what I've been given?

One of my favorite Scriptures is John 10:10, *"A thief comes to kill, steal and destroy, but I have come so that you may have life and have it more abundantly."* God wants us to have an abundant life and to live it to the full.

So many people just can't seem to let go of past failures in their lives. They dwell on them and let them consume every thought. I've beaten myself up countless times for mistakes I made in the past and things I wish I could've done differently. I made poor choices, as many of us do in our lifetime. As a Christian I bring my mistakes to the Lord, I confess them and repent and ask for forgiveness. My sins have been forgotten as far as the east is from the west. If the Lord has forgotten my sins and remembers them no more, why am I letting them consume me and bring me down? Why am I thinking that I'm this terrible person?

I try to remember every morning when I pick up my cross that it's not me but the sin in my flesh that allows the world into my life at times. I need to always be on guard and remember the Lord's hand is always on me to divert me from the path my body and mind often are drawn to. It's so easy to be consumed by life and it happens to me often. Before I realize it, I've let the daily grind and things I have to get done occupy my every thought. I think about bills that need to be paid and wonder at times if I'll ever be at a point where I won't need to worry about bills and making money 24/7. Instead of stopping and looking around at what God has created for me, I look narrowly through glasses that only allow me to see to the horizon. I have to make myself stop and look around and thank the Lord for my life.

If there is one thing I have as a Christian that I didn't have before I knew the Lord, it's a strong sense of conviction. I see and feel the sin before it comes to fruition. I'm so grateful for this, because the Lord will help me hold my tongue and stop before I let myself do something that would not honor God. In a study two weeks ago, my wise brother in Christ, Sylvester, said if you do something and it brings glory to you, it's of the flesh, but if you do something and it glorifies the Lord, it's of the Spirit. That made me really think about the things I do every day. Who gets the glory?

Many Wednesday nights I'm tired and want to just come home and relax and my mind starts to tell me how nice it would be to just stay home and watch a good movie or read. Again I feel God's presence and know I have a Bible study to attend and there's something that I personally need to hear, or better yet, the Lord wants to use me to say something that someone else at the study needs to hear. He uses us in different ways every day, and when I get home from the Bible study, I am so grateful that I attended.

I've started bringing my son Austin, who is 14, to the Bible study every other week when he's with me. He's at the age now that it may not be much fun for him, but I know the Lord is honoring it and doing a work in him without him even being aware of it. He often daydreams and doesn't pay a lot of attention, maybe because the subjects are a little over his head, but I believe he is being touched every week.

My past failures have created a constant burden on me that I pray will someday be forgotten completely. I am overly-paranoid now when I'm in a relationship and have insecurity which I know is not of the Lord but of my flesh. I believe it stems from my past, and even though it's not a part of my life now I still constantly have to get insecure thoughts and feelings out of my mind.

31

CHAPTER

DIVORCE

I DIDN'T PLAN ON WRITING ABOUT THIS AT FIRST, but it's part of my life and part of who I am, so I need to bring it up. It's a bad word in Christian circles, and not many active evangelists out there have gone through it. I certainly didn't think I would be part of the statistic.

When I was 12, my parents divorced. Like every young child who goes through this, I blamed myself and thought that I played a part in my parents not being together still. I remember that time of my life well and the struggles and hard times I went through for years after. Being the oldest of three, I felt like I needed to be strong and show my siblings that everything was going to be okay. I remember having a terrible feeling inside me that just wouldn't go away. I saw my parents struggling even after they separated and as I look back I see myself.

I told myself I would never do this to my children and do whatever I needed to so they wouldn't have to feel the pain I did. It was terrible as I went to a sporting event and had to figure out where I was going to sit, with mom on one side of the gym or dad on the other. How was I going to split up the time and what was I going to say when I had to get up? Seems pretty simple, but for a 12-year-old kid who loved both his mom and dad, it was anything but easy.

I felt guilty for years that I was only getting to spend every other weekend with my father. He was out in the world all by himself away from all of us. I didn't know the details of the divorce, just the ramifications of it. I didn't know the reasons for it for years and still probably don't know all of them, and I don't want to. I do remember the fights and arguments when I was young and those left me feeling pretty sad, but it always got better and we were still a family, all living together under one roof.

The day my parents sat the three of us in the living room of our tri-level home will be ingrained in my mind forever. I remember the talk, the tears, the confusion, and the sadness that followed. I remember the weekends at my dad's apartment and trying to get used to seeing both of them with other people. Seeing them holding hands and being affectionate with someone else left me feeling angry and mad at the other person. Going out to dinner with a strange person was not easy to get used to as we would compare them to our real mom or dad. It took years for me to really be comfortable seeing them with anyone else.

So as my 12-year-long married life started to take a nosedive, I had a sense of *déjà vu*. As hard as I wanted my kids to live in a functional, happy home, I found mine anything but that. We had arguments and disagreements that ended up way too loud. Never did I want my boys to hear arguments like I heard from my parents. I was living out the exact pattern I'd told myself I never would.

When Jesus isn't a part of your life, He probably isn't a big part of your marriage. Growing up in church, I thought I had all I needed in that department. I went through confirmation classes at the Lutheran church and didn't think I needed God in my life to be successful and happy and complete. Yes, I was very wrong, and it took me 32 years to figure it out. Life had completely grabbed hold of me and consumed me.

I was not a cruel person and always had a kind demeanor, but was living life for all the wrong reasons, and looking for happiness in all the wrong places. My wife was working a full-time job at home and putting in long hours to get her career off the ground, and I was teaching and coaching in high school and putting in long hours myself. Raising two boys and getting them involved in every sport we could kept us running in all directions as fast as we could. We ran so fast that we ran away from each other, allowing our lives to pull us in opposite directions. As I said, when God is not at the center of your relationship, you're doomed from the start.

Before we ended it for good we did make a trip to church one Sunday morning. My father had been attending a church in town for some time and had been telling us many good things about it and about how his new relationship with the Lord had completely changed his life. I had definitely seen a difference in him.

He'd been asking us to attend a service with him but we always had a reason not to go. You know—*we had a much too busy schedule to go to church two hours out of our weekend.* So week after week we would turn his invitation down.

This Sunday was different. We weren't doing well and were about to call it quits so we finally said *yes* to my father's invite. It was one of those Sundays that I was certain the pastor was tipped off beforehand that we were coming because he was talking directly to me. Every word he spoke was piercing through my skin and grabbing hold of my heart. I didn't know how to act or feel, but I found myself fighting back emotions I hadn't felt before. I looked around to see if anyone was looking at me because tears were building up in my eyes and I had to get them out before someone did see them. When I looked at my wife beside me, I noticed that she also was affected because she didn't hold it back like I had and tears were flowing down her face.

We left that Sunday in a bit of shock, not really knowing what hit us. But we both did know that whatever it was we needed more of it. So the next Sunday was a no-brainer. We went to church on Sunday morning, week after week, and felt a presence like nothing we had before. It seemed we were being spoken to directly every week.

One Sunday morning, the pastor of the Wesleyan church we were attending invited people to respond to the message to accept Jesus into their lives and let Him take control. It was as if Christ was inside me and told me it's time to take a stand. I grabbed my wife's hand and we both walked to the altar, professing Jesus as our Lord and Savior. It was a magical day in my life and I felt I was floating on a cloud. So many emotions and feelings—and all at once they hit. I knew I was a changed person that day from the inside out.

I was so on fire for Jesus. I just couldn't seem to get enough and learn fast enough—Bible studies every Wednesday night and reading my own Bible every chance I could. My taste in music completely changed and a strong sense of conviction fell upon me. I was indeed a new creation.

"Therefore, if anyone is in Christ, he is a new creation, the old has gone, the new has come!" (2 Corinthians 5:17)

The overwhelming problems we were facing in our marriage seemed to be taken care of one at a time and, believe me, they were overwhelming! Opportunities started to pop up in our lives. I was given a UFC contract, followed by a WWF/WWE contract a year later, and financial worries lessened as my wife's business began to boom as well. She moved up to a sales director and was driving a free company car.

One misconception many people have about Christians is that they no longer have sin or problems in their lives, as if God just doesn't allow it any more. Boy, do I wish that were how it all worked, but the truth is in Romans 3:23, *"for all are sinners and fall short of the glory of God."* We all have a free will and make poor choices every day. We drift away from God's Word and get caught up in the world. Staying grounded in the Word and surrounding yourself with Christian brothers and sisters is a very good defense mechanism, but nothing is seal proof. We can all mess up and often do. We let ourselves believe we're in control and can handle things on our own, whether it be finances, self control, our tongues, or our actions. It's that mentality that gets you off the path and quickly into trouble.

As I started to see the amazing opportunities fall into place for me, I had no trouble thanking the Lord for the blessings. But it wasn't long before I fell flat on my face. I moved out of the house to pursue a WWE wrestling career after being offered a big developmental deal. My wife was not excited about this but we both thought it would be no big deal for me to move away for a few months to learn what I needed to learn and move back home to the perfect life I always wanted—money, fame, and a lifestyle that most only dream about—a WWE superstar.

Well, things didn't turn out just as I'd planned or had been told they would. I found myself in a strange place away from my family, my support group, my pastor, and my accountability partners. I was in a place where I was really on my own.

Most of the wrestlers I befriended were great guys but not very many had a relationship with Jesus and the environment we were in was anything but godly. I found myself falling fast and conforming not to the Word but to the world. I was being swept right into a lifestyle that I saw so much differently. So much corruption was in front of me, and day after day I felt myself being pulled in and not being able to pull myself back.

Days, then months, then a year, and I was far from where I once was, far from the godly man who was on fire for the Lord. My life had become confusing and I had no idea what was going to happen. The pressure of succeeding or being sent home was a constant battle week after week.

To this day, I feel that Jesus pulled back on the rope some at that point in my life and kept me grounded. My WWE career was now just a small chapter of my life and God had me set for bigger and better things. Some of the trials and sufferings I had been through were what the Bible calls the *"refiners fire."*

"Though now for a little while you may have to suffer grief in all kinds of trials. These have come that your faith of greater worth than gold...may be proven greater and result in praise and honor." (1 Peter 1:6-7)

The time I'd spent away had done damage to my relationship once again and what was on the road to recovery was set back largely because of my doings. I was fighting to get back to where I needed to be spiritually. The Lord put Team Impact in my life and that was the medicine I needed for recovery. I was soon on the right path, but the travel continued and the time away was still time away. I wasn't the only one who needed some recovery and I was too blind to see it.

As time continued to run by with Team Impact, I was feeling great with my Christian walk but not as the spiritual leader I needed to be at home. Things were slipping to a place we'd been when we didn't know the Lord. Now that we did, it wasn't supposed to be this hard. Life had once again grabbed hold of us and pulled hard enough to end a 20-year marriage.

As a Christian in this relationship I would have never ended it regardless of the struggles I faced and the challenges that were in our marriage, many that I created. Just because I didn't end the marriage doesn't mean that a good part of the problems that created the divorce didn't come from me. It takes two, and I had my share of faults and issues.

Many think that after becoming a believer, you rid yourself of serious problems and your troublesome past is all of a sudden gone. The truth is that marriage is extremely difficult and needs to be a top priority in every married person's life. You don't have to try to end your marriage—the world will do that for you. You must fight to keep it. For us, Christian counselors and pastors weren't able to pull it back together this time, and I saw a familiar road being traveled.

When I see couples celebrating long marriages, I see more than just a couple. I respect the battles they've won together and the problems they've overcome to make it work. Divorce is the easy road out, it takes a special couple to sustain and fight the battles the world throws at them.

Today I see my boys and I feel the pain they're going through, although it's been several years now. It's easy for me to spot their uncomfortable feelings when seeing me with my fiancé. I'm not a great communicator when it comes to talking about feelings. I don't talk about mine very well and am worse trying to talk to my boys about theirs. I see myself in both of them all the time and I understand the pain does go away with time.

My mother remarried and I have a very good relationship with my stepfather now. As a matter of fact, we're partners and work together almost every day in my real estate business. My father also remarried but it didn't go as well and ended in a nasty divorce after 12 years. He is single now and a strong Christian man who is very involved in his church. I'm close to my father and also work alongside him often when I flip a house or need anything done, as there is not much he can't do. I learn from him all the time and will never have the knowledge he does when it comes to handyman work.

Although I am now a grown man, I still feel my father's conviction when I know I'm in the wrong. And of course I feel my heavenly Father's conviction as well. I pray that my boys will forgive me for the divorce and learn what I hadn't—that it takes a great deal of dedication and that the Lord must be in the middle of the marriage for it to last a lifetime.

32

CHAPTER

FULL CIRCLE

I'm a strong believer that, in time, things always come back around. When I was a high school art teacher—yes, an *art* teacher—I would train at five o'clock every morning and do an hour of cardio, followed by an hour of intense weight training. It was just my schedule and a way of life for me. I would teach all day and head to practice right after school. My days were long: football in the fall, wrestling in the winter, and then I ran a freestyle wrestling program in the spring.

My last couple of years as a teacher was when I began Mixed Martial Arts. The only way I could learn jujitsu and striking was to drive to Denver, 50 miles away. So after practice ended at 6 p.m., I would head to Denver to put in another couple hours and drive back. My days were crazy long and took a toll on my body. I knew this was a big opportunity for me so I had to take advantage of it when I could. This crazy routine carried on for a couple years as my opportunities in the UFC continued.

It's interesting that 11 years after I began this journey in MMA, I'm doing much of the same: training every day, working a full-time job, speaking in schools, and continuing to travel with

Team Impact. My hour-long drives to Denver are better because I travel with one of my old high school wrestlers, who is now, by the way, training to take on the current UFC champion, Brock Lesnar. Shane Carwin started helping me train about five years ago. I would have a big fight coming up and would call him to help me train in the wrestling room.

Shane had gone on after high school to compete in football and wrestling at Western State College. He would soon become an All-American in both football and wrestling. Shane was a late bloomer physically—he put on about 80 pounds of muscle after graduating and became a physical specimen! His is a very similar story to my own as I wrestled 167 pounds in high school as a senior after cutting 20 pounds to get there. Then a few years later in college, I was a 235-pound heavyweight.

I watched Shane compete his senior year at the Conference championships and he just toyed with people to become a Division II national champion. So it was a no-brainer to call him up to help me train and prepare for big heavyweight contenders. He was a little unsure of the whole MMA thing to begin with, but soon became as hooked as I was when he started to learn submissions. Shane is a great athlete and fast learner, so the sport came to him quickly. He trained with me off and on for a couple years and started to compete in small shows that Phyllis and I found for him to break into MMA the right way. Shane began to walk through opponents and not even break a sweat.

As my time became more consumed with traveling, Shane needed to take his training to the next level. I introduced him to Nate Marquardt, another top UFC fighter I had trained with in Denver many times. Nate introduced him to some key trainers in Denver and before long he was part of the Grudge MMA School and training almost every day of the week.

Shane is now preparing for a shot at the UFC Heavyweight belt and is working hard to make that dream come true. The training is intense and I go down with him a couple times a week. Trevor Wittman, the owner of the Grudge Training Center in Wheatridge, Colorado, holds some very intense practices and you can't help but get better every day you set foot in the gym. I became a part of the team a few months ago and see a whole other side to this.

For my first ten years of fighting, I was, for the most part, on my own, training at random gyms, wherever I could find big bodies to work with. But as the sport has evolved, you can't get by that way any longer. Too many fighters are doing just that—eating, sleeping and training—that's all they do. So obviously, to fight at this level you must be trained by the best and in many different areas. The day when a great wrestler could walk into the octagon and dominate is gone. Everyone is trained now and in many different disciplines. A one-dimensional fighter would get his lunch eaten with the caliber of fighters now.

After a tough training session with Shane and the many pro fighters at Grudge, I'm thankful when I can walk out without an injury or being too stiff to move. It's a rough few hours of training, but I understand the importance of it to be successful. No short cuts, just hard work. The Grudge Training Center offers an exclusive pro MMA fighters training time, so we're there with only other professional fighters. All are extremely talented fighters and spar with one another full-speed.

The first practice I attended, I broke my nose from getting punched so many times square on. A month later I had surgery on it so I could breath. A few weeks later, I tore my left bicep in practice by throwing a left hook and extending it. Three weeks later, I was under the knife once again, getting my bicep tendon pulled down my arm and re-attached to the bone.

Shane is rehabbing a bad knee that he tweaked in practice a few weeks back.

After a few months of instruction from the coach, I'm moving and punching 100 percent better. I feel ten times better after a few months of this kind of training, especially being at least a decade older than everyone else in that room. The injuries set me back a few months and I hope to get back to training soon.

33

CHAPTER

SOMETIMES WE LOSE

I STARTED OUT THIS CRAZY OCCUPATION with a bang as I disposed of my opponents one at a time and didn't fight longer than two minutes into the first round. But a streak like that can't continue forever.

For my second big opportunity fighting for the UFC, I took a fight on short notice against a 400-pound opponent—Andre "The Chief" Roberts. I had seen Roberts fight before and was confident I could win. I trained hard and had a solid game plan intact, but sometimes things just don't go as planned. Roberts had a boxing background so I wasn't planning on staying on my feet with the giant for long. I did train on my feet for him and felt okay about my hands.

As the fight began and we started to feel each other out, I began to land almost all my punches. He was much slower than me, so I was able to get inside his punches and land most of mine. I broke his nose in the first 30 seconds of the round and Big John, the referee, actually stopped the fight to let the doctor look at it. They allowed him to continue and it went much the same way as I began to land punch after punch.

At one point, I had Roberts up against the fence and his eyes rolled back in his head. I knew it was only a matter of time so I really turned it up. John started to yell at Roberts, telling him he needed to fight back soon or the fight would be stopped. I continued to land punch after punch on the fence. A few punches later a desperation swing came from nowhere and landed right on my jaw. As my head began to spin, my equilibrium was thrown way off. I believe that was the first time I'd ever been hit on the button and had a really hard time recovering.

I fell to the mat with some sense of what was going on as Roberts pounced down on me. I grabbed a leg and held on tight to the 400-pound monster. We ended up in a scramble once again and I came back up to my feet, still very dazed. Roberts could tell and he landed yet another glancing blow, and I fell back to the mat again. Big John stepped in and stopped the fight. *Wow, what just happened? I was in total control one minute and the next the fight was over.*

I believe this is how most fighters feel after a knockout. It's a terrible feeling because most of the time you feel fine minutes after and can't understand why the fight was stopped. That was my reaction. You can win 100 fights in a row and it's the one you lose that you can't get out of your head. The regrets and second-guessing of your strategy haunts you for years. I can't tell you how many times I've replayed that fight in my head and said if I would have only taken him down it would have been done instead of trying to finish him on my feet.

After 24 professional fights over the last ten years, I have had a few losses and none of them easy to take. Being as competitive as I am, I really dislike losing regardless if I'm in the octagon or playing volleyball in the backyard. When you have that competitiveness in your system, it's difficult to get rid of. Those closest to me see it the most and know how much it really eats me up to lose at anything I do. I believe it's hereditary because my two boys are exactly the same way. They are competitors to the end, and a loss really bothers them. Losing is not always a bad thing as long as you can control your anger and learn from it to make you better.

As a coach, nothing bothered me more than to see a sore loser, someone who threw a fit after a loss, throwing things around, not shaking an opponent's or coach's hand, and storming off, disrespecting his coach, teammates, family, and himself, then having the audacity to blame someone or something other than himself for the loss. I'm hard on myself after a loss but never disrespectful to an opponent or anyone else. That is what I coached to my athletes and my own children—it's just not acceptable.

ONE TUFF ROOM
AT THE GRUDGE TRAINING CENTER IN DENVER

34

CHAPTER

HIGH SCHOOL COACH

AFTER COLLEGE, IT SEEMED TO BE A PERFECT FIT to work at my alma mater. The wrestling program had been in the dumps for several years and coaches came and went just about yearly. I was fresh out of college and had already coached at UNC for two seasons as I finished up my degree. (Yes, I was on the five-and-a-half year program in college.) I felt very comfortable coming in and running a high school team after the experience coaching in college. I also knew the art teacher was getting close to retirement and the timing would be just about right.

I interviewed for the wrestling position and was offered the job. I knew the art position was going to open up halfway through the school year and I'd have a foot in the door if I was already coaching there. I ended up taking a position at the school as a campus monitor for the first half of the year and was hired on as an assistant football coach, which turned out to be a really good move for me as a recruiting tool.

I beat down the halls every day getting any athletic body I could find to sign up for my team. I had an inside track on my football players, as many of them had never wrestled before but were athletes who could be coached. The year before, the team ended the season with only 12 wrestlers and had not won a single match, so it wouldn't be hard to beat. I was on a mission to get a lot of kids out for my program and ended up having 54 kids on the first day of practice. The numbers didn't last long as I pushed them harder than they'd ever been pushed in their lives. My philosophy has always been, you never lose because of being in poor shape, and if you do it's the coach's fault.

The kids who did make it through the difficult practices had no choice but to get better as a wrestler and as a person. Things quickly started to turn around as we began to win dual matches and compete in and win tournaments. It was fun having coaches come up to me after duals and tournaments and let me know what an amazing turnaround the Greeley West program had taken. I am a person who works harder after positive reinforcement rather than being criticized. So the feedback gave me more motivation to work harder and make each of my wrestlers the best they could be.

When your athletes see how much you care and how hard you work they're willing to push themselves harder just so they don't let you down. I had many athletes who achieved levels they probably never before had in their lives and realized they were capable of doing much more than they ever imagined they could.

Each year I would have wrestlers who I really enjoyed coaching and watching become competitors. I remember just about every wrestler I coached over the years and remember their work ethic and how they did. I always wanted to see my athletes go on to college and pursue wrestling, but very few did.

The life lessons most of my athletes learned will last them a long time. Wrestling had a big part in making me who I am today. I learned about discipline and how hard I could push myself, cutting weight and having the willpower to say *no* as I watched my friends eat lunch every day. Discipline came in many forms as most of my friends didn't follow their training rules for sports. My group was athletes, but they wanted to party and impress one another more than take each sport seriously.

It must have been my parents' influence on me that helped me to stay strong and resist the temptations of following the crowd. It made me feel good; being able to stay strong and not blow something I'd promised and committed myself to do. I was somewhat of an easy target as I was the only one who didn't party during the season. It makes me feel much better today as I can look my boys in the eye and tell them I understand the pressures of high school and let them know I was able to say *no* to alcohol and drugs, and I expect them to do the same. Pressures in high school really aren't any different today than they were 20 years ago.

35

CHAPTER

UFC

I WAS INVITED TO THE BIG SHOW before I really knew what to expect, which was probably a good thing. I get asked all the time if I get nervous before a fight. I do know a few fighters who I really don't think get nervous at all but most fighters do get some nerves before a fight. The feeling is different for everyone, I'm sure, but it's near impossible not to get nervous before stepping into the cage. I have periods of nervousness sometimes days before a fight, and then often the day of the fight is a long one. Its amazes me how the Lord takes it from me before I head out to the cage and helps me prepare my mind.

When you train as you should for a fight and have put in the hours, it just makes it all the easier to change the nerves to confidence. There also comes a point when you just want to get the fight over with and take a deep breath.

My first UFC opponent was also debuting in the Octagon as I was and had a bad case of nerves as well. I was told a few hours before the fight that my opponent may not be able to compete, as his blood pressure was way too high. They had to calm him down and allow the doctor to clear him before the fight would happen.

The UFC has changed a great deal since UFC 20, when I first entered the Octagon. We were treated well and put up in nice hotels, but the exposure and venues were a much different environment than what we see today in Vegas. The public still saw the sport as a violent, uncontrolled brawl that was for barbarians. Senator McCain called it a "Human Cock Fight."

The UFC was owned by Bob Meyrowitz, who was always a nice guy to me. He had his work cut out for him in the beginning, as he was trying to get rid of the "No holds barred" reputation of the UFC. Television had banned the sport and it was only available for viewing on a few select pay-per-view channels.

Big John McCartney was the main official and ended up doing all of my UFC fights. I think they wanted him in with the big boys in case something went wrong. Even in UFC 20, the rules and control they had in the cage were different. The old tournament-style UFCs and unlimited fighting times had changed to three five-minute rounds. Blood was treated differently, as were the fast stoppages when an opponent was being mauled.

The UFC was in a transitional period when I fought for them. In UFC 21, the Las Vegas athletic commission attended the event to see if it was a sport they could sanction. So the rules began to be modified and put into a more controlled setting; fights were stopped when an athlete could no longer defend himself intelligently. My first UFC fight only lasted 23 seconds as my opponent tapped quickly as I began to ground and pound.

It's hard to describe what it feels like to have your hand raised in the middle of the Octagon in front of the world. I had my hand raised many times in my wrestling career but it just was not the same. It can be a rush and addictive when you get a taste of that victory.

I'd trained with Bas Rutten for this fight in Denver, Colorado, as he was the main event against Kevin Randleman. Bas liked to train at our altitude to prepare his lungs, and it's a good thing he did because he ended up having a war with Kevin. It ended as a controversial decision and one that Kevin didn't agree with—he went a little crazy after the judges awarded the win to Bas. Peretti had me come out and walk Bas back to the locker room to protect him from Kevin's rage. Little did I know that I would be in the ring with Randleman eight years later, fighting him in the Pride fighting championships.

Fighters know that most injuries happen preparing for a fight, not in the fight itself. I was virtually injury-free for most of my collegiate wrestling career and right up to my third UFC fight. Training at Stars in Broomfield, Colorado, a week before I was to fly out to UFC 23, I took one of my training partners down and heard my right bicep pop as I hit the mat. It was a little painful but I didn't understand the severity of the injury. I ended up practicing for another hour or so with it and then drove an hour back home to Greeley.

That night the pain started to get severe so I called a good friend of mine named Dennis Martin, who was a sports injury trainer that I used often. I went to Dennis's home late that night and asked him to take a look at my bicep. Dennis felt around for my bicep tendon and did a number of strength tests on my arm and quickly came to the conclusion that my right bicep tendon had completely torn off the bone and rolled up my arm. I noticed that my bicep was a bit odd-shaped and much higher than it usually was when I would make a muscle.

Dennis called over the doctor that he worked with, and he analyzed my arm and came to the same conclusion. I explained to Dr. Anderson that night that there was no way I could go in for surgery right away because of the fight only one week away. Against their judgment I did what I could and got on a plane a few days later for my fight. It was my right arm, so striking would be difficult with only a left jab to throw. My game plan was to take my opponent down and go for a submission.

My UFC opponent was Tim Lajcik, a great striker and a very good wrestler. What I hoped to be a quick fight ended up going all three rounds. I had a tight neck weave in the first round but it was put on with my right arm and I just didn't have the strength in it to finish him off. We went three hard rounds and were both exhausted at the end of the fight. I won round one and three, but was called for a low punch in round one so it ended up being a draw, as did the fight. I was frustrated but at the same time relieved that it was over.

An hour after the fight my arm ballooned to almost twice its normal size. The pain was pretty severe and I had my surgery scheduled for the day after I arrived back home. They ended up pulling the muscle back down my arm and drilling a hole in my ulna, pulling the tendon down to it, and tying it off on the other side of my forearm. The surgery put me out of commission for about five months and left me with a lot of rehab to do so my arm would regain its strength and flexibility.

I look back at the fight today and watch as Tim and I were fighting on the ground. Several times you can see my right bicep balled up next to my shoulder. I didn't let anyone at the UFC know about the injury before the fight because I knew I'd be pulled from the fight card and didn't want to lose the opportunity. After the fight, my manager let John Peretti know about it—he was one of the matchmakers for that UFC event. Eight months later I was invited back to fight in UFC Japan.

It would be the first time I traveled outside the U.S. We were treated like royalty in Japan by the fans and press and it was an exciting card to fight on. Tito Ortiz was matched up with Wanderlei Silva. Chuck Liddell was on the card along with several other big names. Back then the names really weren't that big, not like they are today. I was fighting a Japanese opponent by the name of Satoshi Honma, who I knew very little about. I had seen a few of his fights but had little knowledge of his abilities.

The Japanese culture was interesting and so different from what I'd imagined. We stayed in a five-star hotel and seemed like giants among all the Japanese fans. They followed us everywhere, taking photos and asking us to sign pictures they'd already printed up of us. They would come prepared with markers and were always very respectful.

One day as we sat in the lobby waiting for a van to transport us to a media event, several of the Japanese Sumo wrestlers walked through in front of us. I thought we were treated well until I saw the way they were looked upon. I also felt like a really big guy until I stood next to one of those behemoths. They had their hair perfectly done and walked through in long, brightly colored robes. They would lay down the red carpet for each of them as they walked by. It was fun to watch.

Many U.S soldiers were stationed in Japan and attended this UFC fight. I actually had a good friend's brother attend the fight, so I had a good cheering section.

I ended up having another three-round fight with Honma, only my second full three-round fight in my career to this point. It was very one-sided as I took down Honma and controlled all three rounds. It wasn't a fancy fight, but I did a good deal of ground and pound and landed about 20 knees to the side of his head. This was a rule they've since changed; knees are no longer allowed to the head once you're on the mat. He was a tough guy and wasn't about to tap out, so he took a good deal of damage.

Most fighting organizations fly out the next day so I didn't have much time to really experience Japan. It was neat to dine in Japan, as their servings are about a third of what we serve.

I had to order four or five meals to get full and the food in Japan is not cheap. We take things here for granted, like free refills on drinks and big portions. It's not so in Japan. I was amazed to see vending machines on the streets that sold beer. The language barrier was also something new to me, although we had an interpreter with us almost everywhere we went. It made me realize what people from other countries must feel like in America.

After my fight, I was shuffled to the back where the interviews and live media feeds were taking place. It was a great feeling to give praise to the Lord and give Him the credit for my victory and do it in front of the world. God deserves the glory. I understand that God gave me the ability to compete at this level and He can take it away at any time. It's hard for me to see others giving themselves the Lord's credit.

TRAINING CAMP

36

CHAPTER

CROSSROADS

THERE HAVE BEEN SEVERAL TIMES IN MY LIFE that I got to a point and wondered where God wanted me next. When I ended my WWE adventure I was left in a strange place. I really didn't feel like I was to go back to teaching again. A few months later, the Lord opened a door for me with Team Impact. I feel I'm in a somewhat strange place now as I'm only traveling part-time with the team and trying to make a living with real estate sales, public speaking, and MMA fights, when I find one that will work with my schedule and be financially worth my time.

Sometimes I feel like I have my foot in many doors but am not really committing myself and giving my all to any of them. Being a hard worker is not the point, it's that with so many different things going on I'm not focused enough on making one really work. I spend a good amount of time every day asking the Lord for direction and awaiting a sign on which direction He wants me to go. Of course, I want answers right away and after a few months of really struggling with this I get frustrated and confused. God's time is not our time and sometimes the lesson is in how we handle the stressful times. I try to remind myself of this daily, but usually fail, as I find myself worrying about what direction I'm headed.

A big part of me wants to go back to full-time ministry with Team Impact as nothing is more rewarding than sharing the Gospel and winning people to Jesus. The down side is that I would miss a great deal of my son Austin's high school sporting events, and there is just one opportunity for that.

With the economy in bad shape right now the real estate market is in the dumps and house sales are really slow, nowhere near what they need to be to make a decent living from it. School budgets are also taking a hit so the funds they allocate to school speakers is not at the top of their funding list, so my possibilities become numbered.

Like most men, I really worry about being in good financial shape and providing for my family. It's always been a stress for me, especially when times are tough. Most families do the normal cutbacks with spending on entertainment and eating out. I've gone as far as selling cars and downsizing everything possible. Sometimes I feel like I'm being tested, like when Jesus told the rich young ruler in Mark 10:21-22:

> *"Jesus looked at him and loved him. 'One thing you lack,' he said. 'Go, sell everything you have and give to the poor, and you will have treasure in heaven. Then come, follow me.' At this the man's face fell. He went away sad, because he had great wealth."*

I don't want to be as shallow as the rich young ruler who failed the test and lost his salvation because of his love for money and his possessions.

I'm often reminded of another verse in Matthew 6:24:

> *"No one can serve two masters. Either he will hate the one and love the other, or he will be devoted to the one and despise the other. You cannot serve both God and Money."*

When I feel like my possessions are who I am, I'm reminded of that verse and it wakes me up pretty fast. We all like to have nice things and there's nothing wrong with having them, but when they become too big of a piece of your life, you need to step back and analyze what's really important. It's apparent to me when I have to start making sacrifices for my family and cutting everyday things back but I'm still driving around in a $60,000 car, that something is just not right, and I need to make some changes. The Lord always provides for us when we're faithful; it's when we're selfish and our love for material things becomes too important that we will be tested.

It's always been difficult for me to see others prosper financially and have more money than they know what to do with. I feel some people who are hard workers and godly people are deserving of the Lord's blessings, but when I see bad people who prosper, it's sometimes hard to understand. I had firsthand exposure to this when I was in the WWE, and saw the crazy amounts of money many of the athletes were making and the lifestyles they were living. Many of these guys were wealthy financially but very poor spiritually. We all know that's not a rewarding life and usually a short-lived one.

The Lord gives us all different gifts and blessings in this life, so we need to be content and happy with the ones that we receive. For many of us, it takes years to figure out what our real blessings are and how we can use them to make our world a better place to live and to glorify Christ in the process.

A good friend of mine once told me that if what you're doing isn't glorifying the Lord, what is the purpose and why would you do it? That really made me think, and reminded me of the bracelet I used to wear that had WWJD on it. I would always look at it and be reminded of the right thing to do. It was in the uncomfortable times and the times that my flesh wanted to do what the world told it that the WWJD bracelet really helped me and put me into check.

Sometimes it's the simple things in life that keep us grounded and living for the right reasons.

My prayers are to hear from the Lord for direction and help in hard times and situations. I believe sometimes the Lord can be very clear as He speaks to us in different ways. On the other hand, there are times that I really struggle to hear Christ's voice in my life and His answers to my prayers. The answers just don't seem to come and I then try to find my own way and take the reins. It's this dilemma that I find myself in too often. The questions I feel like I need immediate answers to that don't come soon enough leave me taking charge myself and usually running the ball in the wrong direction toward the wrong end zone.

UFC 22 AGAINST TIM LAJCIK

37

CHAPTER

MISSION TRIPS:
SOUTH AFRICA

THE FIRST TIME I TRAVELED OVERSEAS with Team Impact, I went to South Africa on a three-week trip. I didn't know what to expect, just the pictures of Africa I had in my head—poor living conditions, starving children, and women carrying baskets on their heads. Well, some of what I had pictured was very true and some a big misconception. There were parts of Africa called townships that were just that; people living in huts built out of cardboard and anything they could find. Townships were huge with sometimes thousands of people living in them.

There were many other parts of South Africa that were very modern with living conditions no different than most of us have right here in the States. We were put up in a nice hotel and were fed like kings. We dined at great restaurants and trained in nice gyms. The surprising aspect of South Africa was how fast you could go from one lifestyle and living condition to another just a block away. Peddlers were trying to sell handcrafted wood items and just about anything you could think of to make money. Vendors covered the streets in most places and loved the American dollar. We were warned about the dangers of giving anything away, as the local people would almost cause riots to get what it was you were giving away. It was always better to travel with the group than by yourself.

I was able to see things I never had before and perhaps never will again in my life. We went on a safari and deepwater dive with great white sharks that were bigger than the small boat we were in. The group of Team Impact members were great, as they all are, so we enjoyed our time and made the most of our trip. Although the trip was not to just sightsee and play, we were there to share the Gospel and speak to thousands of school kids. We did just that as the presentations were standing-room-only night after night, and the number of salvations was unheard of. We did the feats of strength each night and had the crowd in the palms of our hands. We shared from our hearts and the crowds were ecstatic.

It was an educational trip for me in many ways as I saw hundreds of children with AIDS. It a country filled with strange beliefs I can't begin to understand. But seeing these little children who were so young and innocent with the AIDS virus and a short time to live made my heart sink and go out to them. We were able to hold some of them who were HIV positive yet still in the early stages and didn't have any visible signs of the virus. When we heard some of the stories of how these children acquired the AIDS virus, it made us sick to our stomachs and angry. To steal a poor little child's future and dreams is just so wrong, and to do it for your own selfish reasons just doesn't make sense to me.

In one of the townships we visited, a group had gathered and was performing some kind of ritual around a young lady to cast out a demon. They chanted and danced around her. This was something I'd only seen in movies, but here I was in a small shack witnessing it with my own eyes. I really didn't know what to think, nor did the other team members standing beside me. One of our interpreters explained what was going on and that it had nothing to do with the Christian religion.

On one of our free days between crusades we had the opportunity to go on a safari, which I really looked forward to. A chance to see the Big Five: the elephant, water buffalo, rhino, lion, and leopard. We stayed in a small hut for the night, and it was a little on the creepy side after hearing the stories and being in the wild with all these animals around us. We were warned of snakes and scorpions, so that didn't help me sleep much. It was amazing to hear the sounds of the wild at night.

They cooked each meal for us and the guide took us out in a small Jeep with bench seats, so we were packed in. The guide was very serious as he told us about the dangers and each of the animals we would be encountering on the safari. Many animals I found interesting and loved to watch were not the big five but others we only get to see in zoos here in the States. Big warthogs were all over and very aggressive, giraffes and zebras ran wild in herds, giant alligators lined the river banks, and monkeys were all around.

Most animals we encountered were just pointed out and we continued to drive through the bush, although some we had to find and track with our guide. We were told to stay in the Jeep at almost all costs except for a few instances, especially when looking for the lions. We came upon a fresh kill where the lion had just taken down a zebra, so we stayed at quite a distance and watched the lions watch over and eat their meal. This was one instance where you didn't want to leave the Jeep, as lions don't typically attack a large object like a Jeep full of people but a single person outside the vehicle would be in some serious trouble.

The next encounter we had was with the rhinos. We were given instructions about them and told what not to do. Rhinos, like many in the wild, are very protective of their herd and are amazingly fast. You wouldn't guess that by looking at a rhino but we took their word for it. We saw a few quite a distance from the road we were on and were told by the guide we could go ahead and walk up to some trees ahead to get a better view and take some pictures. As we got about halfway to the trees, a mother and her rhino babies came out from the bush next to the Jeep. I was watching our guide to see his reaction and to see if this was a normal happening. He looked worried as he loaded his big rifle with a bullet as long as my hand. He told us to get behind a tree as fast as possible. Well, this was the wrong thing to say to this group of 300-plus pound guys. They all took off lumbering through the bush looking for a tree big enough to hide behind, which none of them did. One of our team members had his wife along and she fell as she was running for cover. With four giant Christian men you would think one would stop to help her up instead of running right by and over her to get shelter. Lori did make it to a tree, but not with the help of any of the guys.

It was a scary situation and I continued to stay by the guide and watch him for signs. It was apparent that he wasn't comfortable being surrounded by rhinos. One wiggled his ears and made a mock charge at us, letting us know we were much too close for comfort. The bad thing was we had nowhere to go. We ended up waiting it out and finally they cleared away from our Jeep and we all made it safely back. The guide said he had been doing tours for eight years and never had an encounter so close that he had to load his gun.

Later we went on to see the elephants, which was also scary because it was after dark and we had to go by sound, not by sight. We could hear the crackling of trees being trampled and were again warned of the dangers. The elephants are very protective of their herds and will charge quickly to protect them. The African elephants are very large, to say the least, and we quickly cut the lights as a herd broke through the bush ahead. It was amazing to see them in their natural habitat and not in a cage. I will never forget the animals we saw that day and the close call we had.

The cooking will also leave a lasting memory, and I was the only one who was affected by it. We had a two-hour drive after the safari ended to meet a pastor for a future crusade to South Africa at one of the biggest churches in Johannesburg. About 30 minutes into the trip, my stomach began to rumble and cramp and I began to sweat. I was in the back of a big van packed with five 300-pound team members and a video man.

We were in the middle of the desert on a two-lane road and not a rest stop, gas station, or porta-potty for a long way. That's why I was sweating—okay, you know what I mean and you know the feeling. It was bad, really bad, and I was growing desperate as I started to look for trees. Nothing for miles and the road was flat and you could see a long way.

Another ten miles and I was at my limit. I had to do something fast so at the next small bush I saw on the side of the road I yelled to the driver to stop and pull over. I made it to the bush and at that point didn't care about the embarrassment of passing cars or a van full of laughing team members. What made it worse was no one had napkins or tissue on them so I had to rely on the bandana on my head. Not a big deal to most people but it was my favorite bandana and I wasn't about to save it. Wow, another safari experience I won't forget, nor will any of the team members on the trip as it's brought up at opportune times to embarrass me.

You just can't explain a mission trip in a third world country until you experience it. You see things you'll never encounter here in the U.S. and realize just how much we all take for granted. It's a trip all our kids should go on to see how good they really have it, even when they think they have it bad. In 2005, I was able to bring my oldest son, Justin, on a mission trip with me to Australia. It's far from being third world but still an amazing country and it was a great opportunity for him. He was able to help us set up the stage every night and listen to our testimonies. It was a couple of weeks I will always cherish and hope he does too.

India

India was another great mission trip that helped open my eyes to other parts of the world, other cultures, and most of all how much we're spoiled here in America. The daily conveniences we have at our fingertips each day would be life-changing luxuries to people in this country. One of the first things we did was visit a school—not a normal school, but one that was about an hour off the beaten path.

Everything these kids needed was provided right there in their village. They had a well that was used for all their water, which was actually a luxury in India. You and I couldn't drink this water, as it was contaminated with bacteria that would make us very sick. I watched the kids in this community work and was amazed at their discipline and organization. They ate the same food every day, which was the rice they planted and grew in the fields on their land. Huge bags of rice were stacked up, as they cooked big barrels of it each day. The kids waited patiently in line as each was given two big scoops on a metal plate. The next line formed in front of a tub of curry sauce that was poured over the rice.

No one in the village used forks or knives. They used their fingers to pack up the rice into balls to eat it. They didn't have benches or chairs but squatted down on the ground and put their plates on the dirt to eat their meals. It was humbling to watch this and picture my life back home; the fancy restaurants and fast food, my house and the food in my refrigerator. Wow, who am I to ever complain about anything?

Most people in America waste more food in one day than these people were eating for the day. It almost makes me sick to think of how wasteful we are. To this day it really bothers me to see a plate of food left on the table at a restaurant or someone ordering food or a drink and only taking a bite or sip and leaving the rest to go to waste. I'm glad I train as much as I do because I now have this urge to eat everything on my plate and my family's plates so there's none wasted. If there are leftovers, it goes in a doggy bag and is eaten the next day.

As we drove into the villages and looked at the shops, vendors, and peddlers along the streets, it reminded me a little of Haiti. There was no sewage system so we would frequently see people standing on the sides of the road going to the bathroom—another shocker for me. I would hear stories about many of the women who would walk for miles to get water from a well every day. The women in India live a very tough life. We would shake hands with some of the local villagers and the women's hands were rough and calloused.

One thing I liked about this culture was that women were respected and didn't flaunt their bodies. Most Americans see Indian women wrapped up in their shawls and robes from head to foot, not showing any skin but their face and hands, because it's viewed as sacred and only for their husbands to see.

We had to walk a fine line in India as we shared the Gospel. A large percentage of the community is of the Hindu religion and the rest Muslim. Christians comprise a very small percentage of the population and from what we understood, when a Muslim converts to Christianity they are shunned by their families. It was a big deal for a conversion in this country, and I didn't know what to expect as we began to share our faith in Christ.

The five-night crusade was amazing, and each night the crowds grew. People walked for miles to attend, and by the last night 25,000 people walked to attend the event. Thousands responded to the invitation to accept Jesus into their lives. It was a life-changing experience for me and my team members to see God move like He did. You can never put a limit on what God can do.

Hawaii

Okay, Hawaii was hardly a mission trip to a third world county, but regardless it was a week I won't forget, partly because I was able to bring my youngest son, Austin, with me. A wonderful lady named Shauna Castle organized this event for me and another NHB (No Holds Barred) fighter named Doug Evans. The two of us put on a one-hour seminar in the church's Dojo. Yes, you read it right.

This was one of the first churches I'd heard of that put in a Dojo to bring people in and reach the lost. We did a big one-night event and shared the Gospel and then I was able to share God's Word the next morning at the church service. We had a good turnout and many walked forward. What made it really neat was that we followed up the Sunday service with a believers' baptism in the ocean where Pastor Tom, Doug, and I were able to baptize over 20 new believers.

We had one lady paddle up on a surfboard and ask if she could be baptized. I'm not sure I will ever have that happen again, but it was very cool. I've had the privilege of baptizing hundreds of new believers, but never in the ocean. It was amazing!

That year I had two fights in Hawaii—one for the X1 Championship belt that I won and another for Strikeforce, which was nationally televised on Showtime. Not many people get to travel to Hawaii three times in a year. Austin had a great time and was able to see the beautiful islands and experience many things he never had before. It's a beautiful state and one I hope to get back to for ministry and for some R & R.

Anytime I can bring one of my boys with me on a missionary trip it's such a blessing. To see my boys in this environment is a great feeling. We had the opportunity to visit Kauai, which was where the crusade was held, and then we traveled to Oahu for a few days and enjoyed a much different but also beautiful part of the islands. It was much more touristy. We traveled to different parts of the island, climbed mountains, spent time on the beach, and of course, enjoyed Hawaiian food.

It's hard to compare Hawaii with any other place on earth. I've certainly never seen anything close to the natural beauty it holds. It would be different to live in this paradise, but as far as spending a few weeks every year, I could certainly do that.

AUSTIN, SHAUNA, AND I ON HAWAIIAN OUTREACH

CHAPTERS OF MY LIFE

As I reflect on the different chapters of my life, I laugh, I cry, I smile, I frown—I experience all the emotions the Lord instilled in all of us. My life has been blessed beyond measure in all ways. I have lived a life with freedom, love, riches, joy, and comfort. I've been reminded often in God's own subtle ways to look at what I've been given.

The Lord sent me to third-world countries to see the poverty, and to towns right here in the United States to see despair. I've seen the brokenness of people who have no hope, and the false sense of pride from those who have been blessed but credit themselves for it. So why is it that I have wasted so much time in my life worrying and stressing about what the next day will bring? I've known now for 12 years that Jesus has His hands all around me and my life. I understand that He is in control and has the perfect plan for my life and that not a single thing happens without His prior knowledge of it. Yet I waste countless hours of my life worrying about things that have no eternal concerns.

I've always been a guy who wants to provide for my family, like most men, I believe. I live in a nice home, drive a nice car, have three beautiful children, and parents who love me unconditionally. I've been a textbook example of someone who is never satisfied and always wants more. Not just financial things like a bigger house and nicer stuff, but wanting to be at the next level, wanting that break in life that makes everything look easy.

I have always felt like I've been on the edge but never over the top. To me maybe it's failure or never reaching my potential, never going the extra mile to get to the top. I blame myself for not achieving it. I've seen my friends get there or seem to get there—breaking through to TV stardom, or reaching financial security, or getting to a place of complete comfort. The truth is, I don't think there are many people in this world who ever reach that place, regardless of their circumstances.

I see my Christian brothers with peace in their lives, but I'm sure they see that in mine as well. I often wonder if they lay awake at night as I do and wonder about the same things I do. Are they worried about the decisions their teenage kids are making, and stressed about the month's bills and where the money is going to come from to pay them? Do they worry about living up to the Lord's expectations of them, and wonder if they're living the life God has laid out for them?

After being a believer for 12 years now and reading my Bible, listening to sermons, and hearing God's voice, I know the answers to all these things, yet my human brain doesn't seem to allow them to sink in. I continue to worry, stress and, yes, even sin.

I hear Paul's words in Romans 7:14-25 run through me over and over:

"We know that the law is spiritual; but I am unspiritual, sold as a slave to sin. I do not understand what I do. For what I want to do I do not do, but what I hate I do. And

if I do what I do not want to do, I agree that the law is good. As it is, it is no longer I myself who do it, but it is sin living in me. I know that nothing good lives in me, that is, in my sinful nature. For I have the desire to do what is good, but I cannot carry it out. For what I do is not the good I want to do; no, the evil I do not want to do—this I keep on doing. Now if I do what I do not want to do, it is no longer I who do it, but it is sin living in me that does it. So I find this law at work: When I want to do good, evil is right there with me. For in my inner being I delight in God's law; but I see another law at work in the members of my body, waging war against the law of my mind and making me a prisoner of the law of sin at work within my members. What a wretched man I am! Who will rescue me from this body of death? Thanks be to God—through Jesus Christ our Lord! So then, I myself in my mind am a slave to God's law, but in the sinful nature a slave to the law of sin.

Romans 7:25 says it all when Paul asks who will rescue him from this body of death: "Thanks be to God—through Jesus Christ our Lord!" My prayer is that the Lord will allow that peace to fall upon my heart and push that human flesh away a little further.

For those of you who feel some of the same daily stress and pressures from life, may my prayer be passed on to you and may the Father of Heaven reach down upon you and touch your life. And remember what God tells us in Deuteronomy 31:8 *"The LORD himself goes before you and will be with you; he will **never leave** you **nor forsake** you. Do not be afraid; do not be discouraged."*

Although we will be let down in life by everyone around us, there is One who will never let us down—Jesus.

TEAM IMPACT IN INDIA

RANDAL HARRIS AND I
IN VILLAGE IN RANCHI, INDIA

DAISY AND RON'S WEDDING

FAMILY

PROUD DAD

FAMILY